EDUCATION IN TWO LANGUAGES:

A GUIDE FOR BILINGUAL TEACHERS

Judith Walker

University Press of America™

Copyright © 1979 by

University Press of America, Inc.™

4710 Auth Place, S.E., Washington D.C. 20023

All rights reserved

Printed in the United States of America

ISBN: 0-8191-0674-7

Library of Congress Catalog Card Number 78-65847

Acknowledgements

No work on education is ever the product solely of the researchers cited or the author but also of the school children and teacher educators who reacted to the ideas, methods, and techniques. I want to thank the bilingual students of Houston's public schools and colleges for all their input, especially Thelma Arrendondo, Norma Perez, Gladys Wren, and Carmen Villanueva.

Special thanks go to those who inspired and helped me in this field. John Rosales, who introduced me to bilingual education; Sr. Mary de Lourdes Warren who gave me the opportunity to experiment when bilingual teacher education was new; Luis Cano and David Maciel, who taught me about Chicano culture and history and helped me become an honorary Mexican; Seymour Menton, who taught me an Anglo can learn to speak Spanish well; and Sylvia Peña and H. Prentice Baptiste, Jr., who gave me insights into curriculum in multicultural/bilingual education. My assistants at the University of Houston contributed a great deal to the final touches of the manuscript; special thanks go to Andrés Príncipe, Homsi Homsi, and Patti Gregory.

I want to also thank friends and family members who helped me with this work, especially Alexis Palmer for growing up with an absentee mother; Emily Boyd for always encouraging me; and Karen Griffin for being my guru, my model, and my typist.

INTRODUCTION

Bilingual education is one of the fastest growing instructional innovations. In the contemporary United States it is different from the hundreds of universal historical and current examples. There are presently tens of models and a dozen different languages being used in them. Perhaps this is why a recent dissertation found a lack of agreement on bilingual education definition, methodology, and goals among teachers, administrators, and parents.[1]

This guide is designed to outline some basics of bilingual education while leaving specifics open to fit the target population. For example, bilingual education will be defined in the text according to the local situation.

At the beginning of each unit specific learner outcomes are listed. Teacher education or inservice programs may use these in designing bilingual teacher competencies.

Learners attempting to assess their capabilities are to read the objectives. If they feel they are able to do them, they turn to the Assessment of Competencies at the end of each unit, work them, and check their answers with those on the Check Sheet. The Check Sheet may also serve as a unit summary.

Learners who are uncertain of their abilities in the specified areas should read the Comment and the Support before attempting the Assessment.

The Comment is a general overview of the topic while the Support cites scholars who have contributed to the area. Advanced learners or graduate students may be expected to read the original works in greater detail or to report on additional and/or more current support.

For advanced learners and for students who are unable to correctly answer the assessment, a list of additional readings follows each unit.

TABLE OF CONTENTS

ACKNOWLEDGEMENTS	i
INTRODUCTION	iii
UNIT I BILINGUAL EDUCATION	1
Definition	1
Rationale	3
Additional Suggested Readings	9
Assessment of Competencies I	10
Check Sheet	11
UNIT II CULTURAL QUESTIONS	13
Stereotypes	17
Dialects	20
Culture Free Evaluation	24
Suggested Additional Readings	25
Assessment of Competencies II	26
Check Sheet	27
UNIT III DESIGNING CONTENT COURSES	27
Systemic Learning	27
Language Learning in Content Areas	32
Suggested Additional Readings	35
Assessment of Competencies III	36
Check Sheet	37
UNIT IV CONTENT AREAS	39
Language Arts	39
Second Language Learning	43
Math, Science, and Health	50
Social Studies	52
Fine Arts	53
Integrated Teaching	55
Additional Suggested Readings	57
Assessment of Competencies IV	59
Check Sheet	60
APPENDIX A	62
APPENDIX B	67
REFERENCES	78
BIBLIOGRAPHY	83

Unit I

BILINGUAL EDUCATION

Upon completion of this section, you will be able to:

--define bilingual education according to the local situation;

--explain bilingual education in terms of social and personal needs.

Definition

Comment

    Although the definition of bilingual education has changed over the years, there seems to be a growing agreement of it by leaders in the field. The teacher in a bilingual program should have a clear idea of what bilingual education is, not only in theory, but also as practiced in the local district and as idealized by the local community.

    The perceptions of the local community as to the role of the school can be detected in many ways. School board elections, comments by prominent citizens, ideas of school administrators all say something about the way the local community perceives the school. But the most important source for determining the community goals for its schools should come from the parents.

    Parental expression of needs is vital, for not only do parents represent the community, they also know their children better, and in different domains of activities, than do the school personnel. Parents have seldom been given the opportunity to verbalize their school goals and have seldom been given an insight into the findings of current research. A successful bilingual education program requires that provisions be made for an exchange of views and information between parents and educators.

    A definition of bilingual education should also be based on current findings by educators, sociologists, and linguists who study bilingualism. Below are some ideas of leading language scholars and others' definitions of bilingual education. Of course, the definitions given here are general and must change with each local situation.

SUPPORT

The bilingual Education Program, Title VII, Elementary and Secondary Education Act of 1965, as amended in 1967, defines bilingual education as follows: "Bilingual education is instruction in two languages and the use of those two languages as mediums of instruction for any part of or all of the school curriculum. Study of the history and culture associated with a student's mother tongue is considered an integral part of bilingual education."[1]

* * *

Joshua Fishman, a sociolinguist who has contributed a great deal to the study of bilingualism, holds that educators must determine the community's attitudes toward both languages. They must also discover where each language is spoken and the stability of each language in the community.[2]

* * *

William Mackey writes that what is needed is not another definition of bilingual education but a classification of the field to account for possible types of programs. He calls this description a typology.

In order to be of use to researchers, says Mackey, a typology has to be entirely objective and based on criteria that are both observable and quantifiable. Such criteria can be found in the patterns of the distribution of each language when describing 1) the behavior of the bilingual at home, 2) the curriculum in the school, 3) the community of the immediate area within the nation, and 4) the status of each of the languages themselves. In other words, bilingual education, as Mackey describes it, is a phenomenon in four dimensions.[3]

The Statewide Design for Bilingual Education in Texas has six components which comprise a definition of bilingual education.

   I. The basic concepts initiating the child into the school environment are taught in the language he brings from home. II. Language development is provided in the child's dominant language. III. Language development is provided in the child's second language. IV. Subject matter and concepts are taught in the child's dominant language. V. Subject matter and concepts are taught in the second language of the child. VI. Specific attention is given to develop in the child a positive identity with his cultural heritage, self-assurance, and confidence.[4]

Rationale

Comment

One of the reasons bilingual education is not already in full force in this country is that there is considerable pressure from the majority to conform to the dominant culture. Children have been punished when they spoke their native languages in schools that permitted only English.

But allowing children to speak their native language at school is not enough. Bicultural children have trouble with school because of cultural rather than linguistic differences. Children who come from schools in Mexico and who speak only Spanish have less difficulty in schools in the Southwest than do Mexican Americans in the same schools.[5]

Bilingual teachers must appreciate a child's two cultures. This way the child will feel appreciated too, and the school will thus provide an atmosphere where children are seen as individuals and not as stereotypes.

Below are examples of the problems which may arise if a teacher is insensitive to children as individuals with differing cultures and needs.

Besides the social values of bilingual education, there are linguistic arguments for adopting a bilingual program in a school system.

First of all, most linguistic studies have shown that children must have second language instruction at an early age if they are to learn that language easily. In fact, continuing studies show that preschool age is probably the optimum time for second language instruction.

The benefits of being bilingual are many. For children who live in bilingual areas, the reasons are obvious. Those who do not speak English will be handicapped in an essentially English speaking, business-oriented country. But even students who speak English well will benefit from bilingual programs. The millions of dollars spent on foreign language learning for intellectual, travel, prestige, and business reasons are proof that people, especially those in the higher economic classes, prize being able to communicate in more than one language.

Support

Experiments by Robert Rosenthal and Leonore F. Jacobson showed that children act according to the way the teacher expects them to act. The experimenters told the teachers to expect certain children to make exceptional academic gains. They were, however, to be given no special treatment. Actually those children had been chosen randomly and were not exceptional. "The difference, then, between these children and the undesignated children who constituted a control group was entirely in the minds of the teachers."

All children were tested after four months of school, at the end of school, and finally in May of the following year. "The results indicated strongly that children from who teachers expected greater intellectual gains showed such gains."[6]

* * *

The U. S. Commission on Civil Rights on Mexican American education in its second report, The Unfinished Education summarized its findings as follows: "The basic finding of this report is that minority students in the Southwest -- Mexican Americans, Blacks, American Indians -- do not obtain the benefits of public education at a rate equal to that of their Anglo classmates.

"Without exception, minority students achieve at a lower rate than Anglos: their school holding power is lower; their reading achievement is poorer, their repetition of grades is more frequent; their overageness is more prevalent; and they participate in extracurricular activities to a lesser degree than their Anglo counterparts" (pp. 41-42).

They also reported that three-fourths of all Mexican Americans in the eighth grade are reading below grade level and nearly one-half of all Mexican American eighth graders are reading at least two years below grade level. Most dropouts have even greater reading problems.

The third Civil Rights Commission report, <u>Teachers and Students: Differences in the Interaction Between Teachers with Mexican American Students and North Americans or Anglo Students</u>, reveals that teachers questioned Mexican American children 20% less frequently than they did Anglo children. Teachers also failed to accept a correct answer from a Mexican American child 40% more often. Teachers used ideas of Anglo students 40% more often than they did those of the Chicanitos.

* * *

Dr. Clark S. Knowlton, in a speech prepared for the staff of Anthony, New Mexico, schools, said,

> One of the most important criticisms of sociologists and anthropologists analyzing the role and structure of the American school system, is that the majority of our schools emphasize middle class Anglo-American values and practically ignore the languages and cultures of minority groups, and the values, attitudes and ways of life of urban poor. As a result, the schools have become dysfunctional among minority groups and the poor. They do not really educate but are responsible for pushing large numbers of children out of schools, for creating serious emotional and cultural problems that scar for life the personalities of thousands of other students, and for turning out children who lack the linguistic, cultural, vocational, and social skills needed to earn a living, to function as intelligent citizens or to make constructive contributions to American culture.
>
> Other authorities emphasize that there is a growing reliance upon intelligence and aptitude tests by teachers, school administrators, and parents to grade students, and to determine their progress in school, their aptitudes, personality characteristics, and ability to learn.

. . .

> As Spanish is not used in school, and as he is often punished for speaking Spanish during school hours, the Spanish-speaking school child comes to regard it as an inferior language to English. He also feels that he

and his culture are inferior to theirs.
This deeply rooted feeling of inferiority
may often paralyze his intellectual and
cultural potentialities....

Furthermore, there is little in the mass
of reading materials, textbooks, or instructional material that has any meaning at all
to the life of a poverty stricken Spanish-
speaking child. The materials portray a
middle class Anglo suburban world of which
he is completely ignorant.... The child cut
off from his own cultural roots comes to
believe that his people have contributed
little of any value to human civilization.[7]

* * *

Chester C. Christian, Jr. writes that one of the
major aspects of the role of educators is the transmission
of their culture. Their limitations are due to thinking
of that role in terms of the transmission of certain
specialized aspects of this culture which they have ac-
quired through great effort and patience, and regard these
aspects as unquestionably universal. They fail to realize
that these specialized aspects of a culture have no meaning apart from the value system, social system, and
communications system which makes them transmissible.[8]

* * *

Miles V. Zintz in Education Across Cultures
reports,

The mean chronological ages and reading
grade-placement scores for various ethnic
groups in a public school fifth-grade sample,
April, 1960, show the average over-ageness
of Apache, Pueblo and Spanish-American
children to be about one year. The Navajo
children were over-age in grade about two and
one-half years. The retardation in reading
achievement, however, as measured by the
Gates Reading Survey Test, was one and one-
half to two years, in spite of the over-age
in grade status.

It is apparent from data obtained in
1960 that there continues to be one full
year of over-ageness for all minority ethnic
groups. This is not as significant, however,

as the indication that even though the sample
children were over-age in grade, they were
an additional one and one-half to two years
retarded in achievement.... Over-ageness and
retardation must be combined to determine the
full extent of educational retardation.[9]

* * *

Bruce Gaarder draws attention to the difference
between native bilingualism and elite bilingualism.[10]
Children who have to learn English to survive in the
dominant culture have had a different attitude toward
language learning than those whose parents want them to
learn another language for status.

Monolinguals' perception of bilinguals often follows
a similar dichotomy. People who learn a "foreign" language
to study abroad are usually held in greater esteem than
those who are born into families who speak the same language.

Bilingual education may be able to change status attitudes toward language by validating the vernacular through
its use in the classroom.

* * *

Wallace E. Lambert, a psychologist specializing in
bilingualism, writing with G. Richard Tucker, said,
"Bilinguals...are more likely to be aware of the symbolic
nature of language and to separate it from both thinking
and learning."[11] Comparing bilingual program children
with monolingual school children in French Canada, they
found that "by grade 5, the (bilingual) children generally
perform better on a comprehensive English-based measure
of verbal intelligence than do the (monolingual) controls.
In terms of creativity, the experimental children perform
as well as, or better than, the controls" (p. 91).

* * *

Wilder Penfield's studies have shown that in the part
of the brain that develops after birth, the uncommitted
cortex, there is a section for the native language, the
"speech cortex," and a section for the perception of the
world, the "interpretive cortex." If children learn a
second language they know to be different and separate
from the first language, the second language is registered
in the perception section of their brains in the same way
the native language is registered in the native language
section.

Penfield's studies suggest that the ages eight to
twelve are the years the uncommitted cortex begins to

lose this ability and finally becomes unable to accept
formative materials. From this time on, a person perceives
the world and language according to the formulae estab-
lished in the interpretive cortex. The children who are
fortunate enough to have a second language space reserved
in the interpretive cortex are able to learn any other
language as they did the first and second languages. The
bilingual child thus has a tremendous language learning
advantage. And, for second language acquisition, the
very young child has a clear advantage.[12]

SUGGESTED ADDITIONAL READINGS

Carter, Thomas P. *Mexican Americans in School: A History of Educational Neglect*. New York: College Entrance Examination Board, 1970.

Christian, Jane and Chester C. Christian, Jr. "Spanish Language and Culture in the Southwest," in Joshua A. Fishman, et al. *Language Loyalty in the United States: The Maintenance and Perpetuation of Non-English Mother Tongues by American Ethnic and Religious Groups*.

Forbes, Jack D., ed. "Education, the Continuing Struggle," Chapter V in *Aztecas del Norte: The Chicanos of Aztlan*. Greenwich, Conn.: Fawcett, 1973. pp. 206-46.

Gaarder, A. Bruce. "Teaching the Bilingual Child." *Modern Language Journal*, XLIX, 164-75.

Saville, Muriel R. and Rudolph C. Troike. *A Handbook of Bilingual Education*. ERIC document ED 035 877. Chapter II.

United States Commission on Civil Rights, *A Better Chance to Learn: Bilingual Bicultural Education*. Washington: U. S. Printing Office, 1974. Spanish edition, *Una mejor oportunidad para aprender: La educación bilingüe bicultural*.

Troike, Rudolph C. & Nancy Modiano, eds. *Proceedings of the First Inter-American Conference on Bilingual Education*. Arlington: Center for Applied Linguistics, 1975.

Assessment of Competencies I

In order to prove that you have the competencies listed at the first of this unit, you must complete all of the following according to the criteria stated:

1. Conduct a survey of at least five sets of parents of children who attend school in the local district. Find out what they would like for their children in the schools and what language needs their children have.

2. Analyze the community according to Fishman's criteria.

3. Write a definition of bilingual education that fits the local district and contains the elements described in this unit.

4. Explain to a parent or to a fellow student playing the role of a parent why his/her child will benefit from the bilingual program you just defined. Include social, psychological, and linguistic reasons.

Check Sheet

You may proceed to Unit II when you have fulfilled all these criteria completely. You may add more material to the following required data:

1. The community must be described by indicating which language is more prestigious, what citizens feel about the other language, where each language is spoken (at home, church, school, etc.), and what changes are occuring in each language. To describe the changes that are occuring in each language, you should note whether new speakers continue to enter the community, whether there is contact with the mother country, and how many generations continue to speak the language.

2. Your answer to this question is correct if you got a response from the parents you interviewed. If any parents were unable to answer your questions, restate them, making sure you are not including technical terms and that you communicate with the parents in their preferred language.

3. In your definition you must incorporate your answers from #1 and #2. Culture, native language, second language components must be included in your definition as well as the idea that instruction of concepts takes place in both languages.

4. In your explanation, emphasize the positive aspects of bilingualism such as creativity, ability to communicate with more people, learning in one's native language as well as in the second language, etc. Any comments with possible negative interpretations, such as dropout prevention and elevating self esteem, must be put in general terms. Do not suggest that their children are likely to drop out. You must include statements on the advantages of early second language acquisition. Describe the program to the parent, and explain how it fits the community.

Unit II

CULTURAL QUESTIONS

Upon completion of this unit you will be able to:

- --Demonstrate recognition of any internalized negative attitudes or prejudices that may interfere with or impede support of bidialectal and/or bicultural children;

- --Demonstrate knowledge of the local dialects and accept them as means of communication;

- --Review evaluation instruments, noting culture bias.

Stereotypes

Comment

Many people find it easier to deal with the world by classifying objects by groups and subgroups. Some people do the same to humans, grouping them in order to try to classify them more easily. To many, the expression "you're my kind of people" is a compliment. The way races and ethnic groups have been categorized on the basis of color is one example of such a grouping.

Categorization puts pressure on minorities from two sides. On one hand, minorities are becoming increasingly vocal, protesting the stereotypes that haunt them. Some commonly heard stereotypes are that Mexican Americans live in extended family situations; that Blacks have a lot of rhythm; that women are always weaker than men; that the poor are under less pressure and are, therefore, happier than the rich. While each statement may be true of one individual, it may just as easily be untrue.

The other side of the problem for minorities is that at the same time that they are combating stereotypes they are also attempting to define an essence which separates them from the dominant culture. Often this can be an exaggerated effort to build self-esteem. At other times such a definition is prompted by a genuine search into a cultural heritage. Many young Jews went to Isreal to attempt to find their essence in the kibbutz. A Chicano publishing company awarded prizes to literature written by Chicanos; most prizes went to those works that described traditional Chicano life. The revival of the African dress and names were also a part of this movement.

Teachers can become caught in the middle of this dilemma. The key issue here is that most bicultural people in this country defy classical sociological classification. No longer can people such as William Madsen[1] fill a book with stereotypes and call their work social science without being criticized by scholars of all ethnic groups. Instead of studying such works, teachers must learn to read critically as well as to sensitively observe the lifestyles of each of their students.

There is an oft-cited case of the school nurse who urgently called the Mexican American mother about her sick child. The nurse got no decided answer because the mother was accustomed to her husband making all the decisions. The moral of the story used to be that the nurse wasted time and should have called the father first. This sort of example continues to be cited at the same time that urban life prohibits such a situation. Urban women are expected to assume more and more decision-making responsibilities, even in traditional families. The new moral of the story should be that the nurse should get to know the families so well that he or she knows whom to call about what.

In most bicultural settings the teacher from one culture is not expected to participate fully in the other culture. For instance, many Anglos overdo when they learn that many members of Hispanic cultures touch more. The embrace that comes spontaneously with a member of one's own ethnic group may be stilted when offered by an outsider.

Or consider the teacher who, after a day at the chalkboard, touches a Chicano baby's face so that the child will not get <u>mal (de) ojo</u>, a colic-like disease strangers can give if they do not touch the baby. Observing first of all if the parents are apprehensive could have told the teacher whether this particular family believed in the <u>ojo</u>. If so, a quick brush to the baby's foot may have been sufficient. An open mind and tactful questions lead to a learning situation for members of both cultures.

<u>Support</u>

Overcompensating for lack of knowledge often leads to stereotyping. One such example is Celia Heller's attempt to make school officials recognize the cultural differences of Chicano school children. In presenting her case, she resurrected tens of stereotypes that might or might not fit each particular child. These included that

-14-

Chicanos are among the least Americanized of the minorities; are an unusually homogenous ethnic group; have a foreign accent; have large families, which hinder progress; are traditional; are overindulgent with their sons, which leads to the boys' lack of achievement; are fatalistic, lax and undisciplined; and do not stress intellectual effort.

Heller's worst mistake was to proceed to the conclusion that Chicano youths who most accepted their parent's socialization were the ones most likely to be juvenile delinquents! This conclusion was based on the stereotypes of machismo (overemphasized masculinity to Heller) and pride. This led her to believe that those Chicanos who most accepted these values would try to prove themselves through gangs and, therefore, become delinquents.[2]

* * *

One of the most pervading stereotypes of minorities is their passivity. Even Robert Kennedy, who was in many ways sensitive to minorities' needs, referred to Mexican Americans as "gentle revolutionaries." Chicano history is full of violent protests of discrimination, all of which contradict such a term.

A text on teaching reading to minorities demonstrates by its title another major stereotype. It is called <u>Emerging Humanity: Multi-Ethnic Literature for Children and Adolescents</u> by Ruth Kearney Carlson (Dubuque: Brown, 1972). Although a useful book, the title continues the timeless view that those who are different are not or have not been quite human until discovered by the majority.

* * *

To combat the view of minorities as passive and less than human, Herminio C. Rios wrote, "and if it is true that the scope and magnitude of activities are unequaled in the history of the Mexican American, it is also true that such achievements are never spontaneous, but necessitate precursors." Then he cites Juan Gomez, a precursor in 1883 of Cesar Chavez; the New Mexico insurrection of 1946 as a precursor of the revolt led by Reies Tijerina in 1967; Manuel Gamio, who in the 1930's described the life of the Mexican immigrant; and others.[3]

* * *

One scholar who has done much to condemn the practice of stereotyping, especially of the Mexican Americans, is Octavio Romano-V. He decries not only the work of Ruth Tuck, Lyle Saunders, Munro S. Edmonson, Florence Kluckhohn,

Celia Heller, and William Madsen, but also those Chicano social scientists who themselves perpetuate these erroneous classifications, "Thus Julian Samora and Richard A. Lamanna, like Heller, Madsen and the others before them, place the final cause of social conditions upon the Mexican-Americans themselves. In doing so, they also commit the fallacy of equating economic determinism with cultural determinism."[4]

* * *

The theme of economic determinism is one echoed by leaders in ethnic groups trying to free themselves from persisting stereotypes. They are careful, however, not to accept the equally stereotypic "culture of poverty" described by Oscar Lewis. Lewis wrote that there are characteristics of poor people that are noticeable in all economically developed countries. These include reliance on the extended family, present orientation, lack of community involvement, early sexual experimentation, little intellectual endeavor, and fatalism, among others.[5]

Teachers must be careful of such gigantic schemes, for each person develops as an individual. The economic question does enter in many ways. For instance, children who live in homes without running water may not be as clean as those who can bathe every day, although many children who could bathe everyday do not. Also, a home that is crowded or poorly lit will be a difficult environment for completing homework assignments. A child who has to work after school may be too tired to be an attentive pupil. And those who ate little for supper and/or nothing for breakfast may appear listless in the classroom. The difficulty for those dealing with minorities is to look at each child. Just because many Puerto Ricans, for instance, are poor does not mean that they will perform badly in school.

* * *

One social scientist, David Lopez-Lee, has suggested that cultural differences are vital and must be taken into consideration. To develop a description of cultural values and still avoid stereotypes, a social scientist could measure each outstanding characteristic of both cultures. A comparison could then be made as to whether there was a statistically significant cultural difference for each characteristic. Dr. Lopez-Lee believes a need is indicated "for a conceptual framework that maximizes accuracy with regard to the personal inferences one makes concerning group differences."[6]

The problem would not be solved, however, if each teacher attempted to fit even this model onto a particular group of students. Such a model would be used for a needs assessment, cultural awareness lessons, application to funding sources, and for other general, district-wide uses.

* * *

All stereotypes hurt those who are the recipients of the typing. About half of all bilingual pupils are girls. Women on Words and Images, a feminist group, studies stereotypes of women. When they surveyed 144 elementary readers from 15 major series, they found:

> 900 stories with a boy as a main character.
> 344 stories with a girl as the main character.
>
> Boys are portrayed as active and independent.
> Girls are portrayed as passive and fearful.
>
> 69% of the women are known only as "Mother."
> Many of them are pictured in the background
>   or through the kitchen window.
>
> 131 biographies of famous men.
> 23 biographies of famous women.[7]

Dialects

Comment

A dialect is a variety of a language. Generally, people are able to understand dialects of the same language. For instance, the Beatles, who spoke with a dialect from Liverpool, England, were understood for the most part by teenagers in Alabama who spoke American Southern dialect. Chicano, Puerto Rican, and Cuban youths travel to Spain and find that there might be a different word for the same object, but that the vocabulary and slightly different pronunciation are the only significant differences between Castillian and American Spanish.

Often people who do not speak two languages or who speak the minority language only slightly, perpetuate the myth that the dialect is "bad." This is especially true for the Spanish-speaking, probably because Spanish is the most-studied language in the United States high schools and colleges. People who learn to say "¿Cómo está usted?" complain that native speakers do not speak "good Spanish" when they hear a Cuban or Puerto Rican say "¿Q'hubo?" or a Mexican American say, "¿Cómo amaneciste?"

The problem persists in French-speaking areas also. Continental French and Belgians complain that the Canadians and the Louisiana Cajuns do not speak "good French." The complaint is similar to that the Latin Americans and Spaniards have of Southwestern United State Spanish because it developed as an isolated language which grew under different influences.

Of course, as the American languages developed they had little contact with the languages of the motherland; some geographical areas had more contact than others. Some new terms, especially words for flora and fauna, developed due to the new environment. With the immigration of English speakers, an English word was often available to fit a new object or experience. On the other hand, terms that became old fashioned in the Old World continued to be used in the New World.

English speakers can appreciate the feeling Europeans have when hearing American dialects by understanding their own feelings when they hear "hillbilly" English. No matter how educated that speaker, standard American dialect speakers often classify that person as ignorant. It is interesting to note that Shakespearean scholars have studied the speech of the mountain areas of the southern United States because these people, isolated from other speakers, retained a language similar to the English used by Shakespeare. Similarly, Chicano students of <u>Don Quijote</u> might find that the old knight speaks quite a bit like their grandparents.

There are arguments on both sides for the use or not of the local dialect in school. Since children must learn to read in the language they speak fluently, there can be no debate that whatever the child speaks at home must be the <u>beginning point in the bilingual classroom</u>.

Whether the language is then developed by adding standard dialect terms depends on the desires of the community. One element to be considered and discussed with parents is that many more materials are available in the standard dialect than in the local dialects. Also, as the world shrinks due to communication developments, children who learn to express themselves in the standard dialect will be in a position to communicate with people from many lands. This is especially true in the Southwest United States and in the cities, where Latin American immigrants arrive daily. The prestige of the standard dialects should be considered. An educated person is expected to speak the standard dialect. To not give children the opportunity to learn the prestigious dialect is to not prepare them for a discriminatory society.

On the other hand, parents who live in an area where they never use nor hear the more prestigious language may not want their children to learn a strange dialect. Teachers should be open to accept this valid point.

If the school district decides that standard dialect will also be taught in the bilingual program, teachers must be very careful to establish that one dialect is not superior to the other. There is already that feeling among most bilingual Americans because of the prestige factor. How much better for a teacher to say (all in Spanish) as he/she holds a picture of a sheep, "In my house I call this a <u>borrego</u> (Southwest term). Is that what you call it? Well, in the story they call this animal an <u>oveja</u> (standard term), so now you know two words for it."

There are several subtle ways one language comes to be considered more important. When the teacher goes into the hall and begins speaking English or when children are scolded in French but have lessons in English, or when the Chinese culture period ends and the real work begins in English, all relay the message that English is the real school language.

Support

Ethnic pride can heighten the value of that group's dialect. For instance, French volunteers are available to Louisiana bilingual programs. However, in some districts, only Cajun French dialect is allowed to be used in the classroom. The volunteers from France cannot speak continental French to the Cajun students.[8]

* * *

Language consists of symbols for items and also for feelings. "Thin" is not as emotionally laden as "skinny," but it is even nicer to say "slender." In an attempt to see what emotions were carried with language in a bilingual, bidialectal community, Wallace Lambert devised a study in which bilingual people were taped reading passages in both languages. One section was all in Canadian English and one section all in Canadian French. The subjects were to listen to the tape, then describe the people who were talking. The subjects did not know that the samples were the same people speaking both languages. The general, the English-speaking listeners rated the women speaking Canadian-French as more intelligent, ambitious, self-confident, and possessing more integrity but shorter than the same women speaking English. However, the English-speaking listeners rated the men speaking English as taller, more affectionate or kinder, and more sincere and conscientious than when they were speaking French. All Canadian-French speakers were considered more religious by the English listeners.

When another group of Continental French women speakers were judged, they rated even higher than the French Canadian women. One surprise in the study was that the Continental French male speakers rated equally with the English speaking males, except they were considered more religious. Also women listeners felt that the Continental Frenchmen were less likeable and less sincere than the same men speaking English.

Another significant aspect is that Canadian French-speaking listeners rated Continental French speakers more favorably and French Canadian speakers less favorably than they did the matched English speakers. The exception was that French Canadian women judged French Canadian male speakers more competent and more socially attractive than the same men speaking English.[9]

The dialect triggered stereotyped responses even though the same person was reading different dialects, and even though logically one can know very little about people listening to them read.

*   *   *

In his doctoral dissertation[10] Gus Trahan showed that, no matter how experienced they were, teachers of all ethnic groups tended to stereotype Mexican-American and Black women. The rate of their willingness to stereotype was, however, related to their overall open or closed mindedness.

Culture Free Evaluation

Comment

There are few standardized tests on the market which are not culturally biased, even though some claim to be. As a rule standardized tests are unfair except to white, urban, middle class students.

None of the I.Q. tests on the market are culture free at this time. In fact, if I.Q. is a measure of what people observe around them, there is a strong argument that I.Q. must have an inherent cultural orientation.

Standard I.Q. tests translated to Navajo, for example, will do very little more for the student than if they were in English. In fact, they may do harm, because whose who do not understand the culture base of I.Q. are likely to use the low test score against the child to an even greater degree, claiming that the child tested "mentally retarded" even in the vernacular.

The first I.Q. test was designed to single out the retarded. Since then that same test or versions of it have been used for many purposes. There is even an organization for high I.Q. elitists. An now parents can buy books to train their children to do well on I.Q. tests.

I.Q. tests do the classroom teacher ABSOLUTELY NO GOOD. If I.Q. scores are included in students' folders, they should be ignored as indicated by the Rosenthal and Jaciobsen study discussed in Unit I. If all students were considered potential "spurters," they would achieve much more than if teachers looked at their scores. For curiosity's sake teachers might look at the children's scores after assigning final grades. They may be surprised to find they have a classroom full of "over" achievers.

Other standardized tests, such as those which measure reading level, are often designed as badly as I.Q. tests but are usually less damaging to a child. After all it is a temporary score, while you have to live with your I.Q. all your life. You can work harder and change a reading score, while I.Q. is supposedly inherent.

Bilingual teachers should protect themselves, their programs, and their students from those who would measure program success by reading level scores. Children who are not ready to begin English readers certainly are not able to read second grade English level on a test, even though they may be in third grade.

Some of the worst damage has been done to speakers of Black dialect English. Due to ignorance of Black language patterns or even simple linguistic theory, school personnel consider these children as speakers of "bad" English and do not let them learn to read first in their own dialect before beginning standard English readers. These students then show poorly on standardized reading exams. Statistically, Blacks as a whole do even worse on reading level than do Spanish bilinguals as a group.

To prevent test discrimination, a coalition of Black, bilingual and knowledgeable English monolingual parents and teachers is more apt to be able to change school policy than one of those groups. Bilingual teachers are in a position to advise or even spearhead such a coalition.

Support

One group making excellent progress in the struggle to do away with culturally biased tests is the Bay Area Bilingual Education League. BABEL held a workshop on multilingual assessment in which participants reviewed 13 of the most commonly used tests in bilingual education projects in California. The group was successful not only in preparing those reviews but also in establishing that many people administering the tests did not know the intended use of the tests and, in fact, admitted knowing very little about them at all.

The workshop also investigated criterion-referenced tests, which proved to be the most promising. This type of test is an achievement test which assesses a specific criterion behavior described in an instructional objective. The assessment is made on the basis of performance itself rather than on comparing performances of others in the group.[11]

Part 4 of their report includes a Neo-Piagetian approach to intellectual assessment by Edward DeAvila (pp. 65-105). The model is intended for those concerned with Piaget's theory that children demonstrate readiness at differing stages and in various ways. In this test children will show whether they are ready to learn a certain principle; the test will not be a mark on the children's permanent record.

* * *

Feminists are also reviewing tests with an eye to stereotypes. Pauline S. Sears and David H. Feldman reviewed studies of standardized achievement tests. They reported that several studies showed that boys did significantly better on math achievement tests than their school grades would indicate they should. The authors felt that this showed a teacher bias toward boys' low performance in school.[12]

Similarly, Carol Tittle reports, "Recent research suggests that the manner in which psychological measures in the vocational occupational area are presented and interpreted for women closes options to women and reinforces sex-role stereotypes."[13] For instance, on one common vocational test, women are unable to show interest in premed, pharmacy, or dentistry. Tittle continues by showing that studies indicate that high school women with atypical career goals are counselled by women and men alike to stay out of those male areas.

* * *

Manuel Ramirez reports that his studies show that test results are affected by who gives the test and the manner in which they give it. For instance, his study indicates that Mexican American children who accept many Mexican values do better in a situation where the examiner is known, gives support, and interprets test performance as achievement for the class rather than for individual achievement. The Chicanitos also did better in a relaxed atmosphere where time was not a factor. Anglo children did best when the last two factors were reversed.[14]

* * *

A psychometrist who worked in a city school enrolling Spanish-American children stated, "Several counselors have mentioned, and I have had the same experience, having a Spanish-American child misinterpret the question on the Wechsler Intelligence Scale for Children, 'How many ears do you have?' The child translates literally in Spanish what you are saying and thinks that you have asked 'How many years do you have?' (How old are you?) He will answer 'seven,' 'eight,' or 'nine,' as the case may be."[15]

Suggested Additional Readings

Burma, John H., ed. *Mexican-Americans in the United States: A Reader*. Cambridge, Mass.: Schenkman Publishers, 1970.

Cabrera, Y. Arturo. *Emerging Faces: The Mexican-Americans*. Dubuque: Brown, 1971.

Emma Willard Task Force on Education, "Consciousness-Raising in the Classroom." *Sexism in Education*. 3rd ed. Minneapolis: The Task Force, 1972. pp. 33-34.

Juhl-Joya, Paul C. and Juan Rosales. *Some Thoughts, Some Activities: Sensitivity Experiences for the Teacher of Mexican American Children in the Elementary School*. Mimeo.

Mercer, Jane. "Multicultural Assessment Procedures for Chicanos in Public School," Paper presented at the First Annual International Multilingual Multicultural Conference, San Diego, April 1972.

Montiel, Miquel. "The Social Science Myth of the Mexican American Family," in Octavio Romano-V., ed. *Voices*. Berkeley: Quinto Sol, 1971. pp. 40-47

Moreno, Steve. "Problems Related to Present Testing Instruments," in *Voices*. pp. 135-39.

Palomares, Uvaldo and Miquel P. Trujillo. "Examination of Assessment Practices and Goals and the Development of a Pilot Intelligence Test for Chicano Children." First Quarterly Project Report, Office of Economic Opportunity Grant. Washington: OEO, October, 1971.

Wolfram, Walt and Ralph W. Fasold. *The Study of Social Dialects in American English*. Englewood Cliffs, N.J.: Prentice Hall, 1974.

Assessment of Competencies II

1. List five stereotypes you have heard about women that you do not believe.

2. Now list five you think are accurate.

3. List five valid characteristics of all members of the minority group you work with.

4. a) Listen to a tape your friends or instructor prepare of target dialect speakers from all walks of life. Write down generally if you would be comfortable speaking with each person, how much education each person has and how you picture each one physically.

or

b) Obtain a copy of Easy Klein, What is Prejudice? Multimedia kit by Warren Schloat Productions, Pleasantville, New York, 1969, and do the exercises.

5. Locate a copy of a common standardized test and review it for the ethnic group you work with, using BABEL guidelines in Appendix A. Any other pertinent information may be added.

Check Sheet

1. This is a personal answer, but you must have five qualities that all women are supposed to have. You may include that they are natural mothers, are silly, moody, intuitive, passive, etc.

2. There is no such thing as an accurate stereotype. Teachers must look at each person as an individual. Any answer here requires you to recycle the "Stereotype" section.

3. There are no characteristics that can describe a whole ethnic group. Not all Native Americans speak an Indian language, not all French Canadians are Catholic, not all Cajuns live in Louisiana, etc. Any answer requires you to recycle through the "Stereotypes" section.

4. a) Remember that the only thing you can tell from listening to an unknown speaker is what your own feelings are. If you discover you have positive or negative feelings (and most people do), think why and concentrate on intellectualizing those feelings.

    b) Answers on product.

5. Since the answers here depend on the standardized test, it is impossible to put all answers here. However, you must include answers to all appropriate points on the guideline. If you selected one of the 13 tests reviewed by BABEL, you may check your answers with their report.

Unit III

DESIGNING CONTENT COURSES

Upon completion of this chapter you will be able to:

--define systematic instruction.
--explain the advantages of programmed learning.
--design curriculum so that each concept is taught in both languages as native languages and in both languages as a second language.

Systematic Learning

Comment

Systematic instruction is one of several terms that is used to indicate a type of instruction in which the overall program goals are considered by professional staff. Individual teachers choose or are assigned competencies that children in each level should attain in order to achieve the program goals. Each teacher then designs objectives to develop pupil competency in the specified areas. Objectives can be clustered by similar levels or under a theme. The teacher then plans activities to aid the students in fulfilling those objectives. The cluster of objectives under a theme, the activities, and an evaluation of the student are all components of a module. This term gives rise to a synonym of systematic instruction, modular instruction.

One of the bases of the systems approach is that learning is defined as changed behavior. To test whether learning has taken place, the examiner should look to the behavior which indicates the desired change.

For instance, if students are to learn about the heritage of the Filipino American, teachers will state the objectives in terms that they can observe. Some examples might be. "you will write a short paragraph in which you describe some historical commonalities of Americans of Phillipine descent". "Working in a group, the third grade student of De Zavala School will present a play representing at least one event that affected the lives of many Filipino Americans." The objectives can be written in either the second or third person, but using the "you form" personalizes the lesson.

Not only must the objectives be specified in assessable terms, they must also be announced to the students before attempting the work. It is a basic assumption in the systems approach that students must know what is expected of them before they can fulfill the objectives.

Realizing that each child is an individual with unique needs, educators may individualize the system by allowing students to choose among activities that lead to the same objective. Students with varying linguistic and cultural needs should be expected to attain similar levels of competence eventually.

Another term associated with systematic instruction is mastery learning. Bloom[1] found that virtually all students in regular classrooms were able to master the lessons if given enough time. While there may be some lessons that require time limits, most modules should provide recycling activities for students who do not attain mastery the first time through the module. Recycling activities may use the other language, if the objective is not language specific. They may provide alternatives that more nearly approximate the student's learning style. They may merely be motivating activities or opportunities to think about the problem in greater depth.

The evaluation is important for two reasons. Obviously it tells the student which objectives need further work and which they have mastered. But it also tells the teacher how effective the module has been. Most teachers modify modules with the special needs in each group of learners. The evaluation must ask students to demonstrate their abilities as outlined by the module. If the evaluation does not measure what the module developed, assessment of student progress will be impossible.

Many teachers complain of how time consuming a systems approach is to prepare. There is no answer to this except that, instead of trying to systematize all lessons in one year, teachers can begin slowly adding a few modules per year. Also, trading modules with colleagues multiplies the number of modules in each teacher's access. Teachers can also request inservice time be spent systematizing lessons and exchanging the finished projects. With time and experience, preparing systematized lessons comes much more easily.

Modular instruction can contribute to each child's self esteem. It puts the responsibility on the student to carry out the lesson, yet it frees pupils from failing.

Support

When Dr. Manuel Ramirez[2] gave the Thematic Aperception Test (TAT) to Mexican American school children, most of the children in the study felt insecure in school. They perceived teachers as punitive. Other tests comparing Mexican American with Anglo pupils found the majority of the Chicanos in the test to be more and more fearful of criticism than the Anglos taking the same test.

Bicultural children are often insecure because of demands made of them by the clash of cultures. Dr. Ramirez suggests that parents may have different values from school personnel, languages may conflict, Anglo classmates may perceive Mexican American teens' respect for parents as weakness and dependence.

Systematic learning provides some security in the school curriculum for all children. Students know where they are going and that if they do not grasp the concept at once, they can try another means until they do understand. For bicultural students, a secure classroom may be a place to gain strength to face the conflicts in society.

Many teachers argue that there is nothing new about the systems approach. There is really not much new in the individual parts. Putting the parts into an integrated system is new to many, however. Technically the instructor should be able to diagram any lesson to describe the integration of all activities. Following is an example of that check for one system:

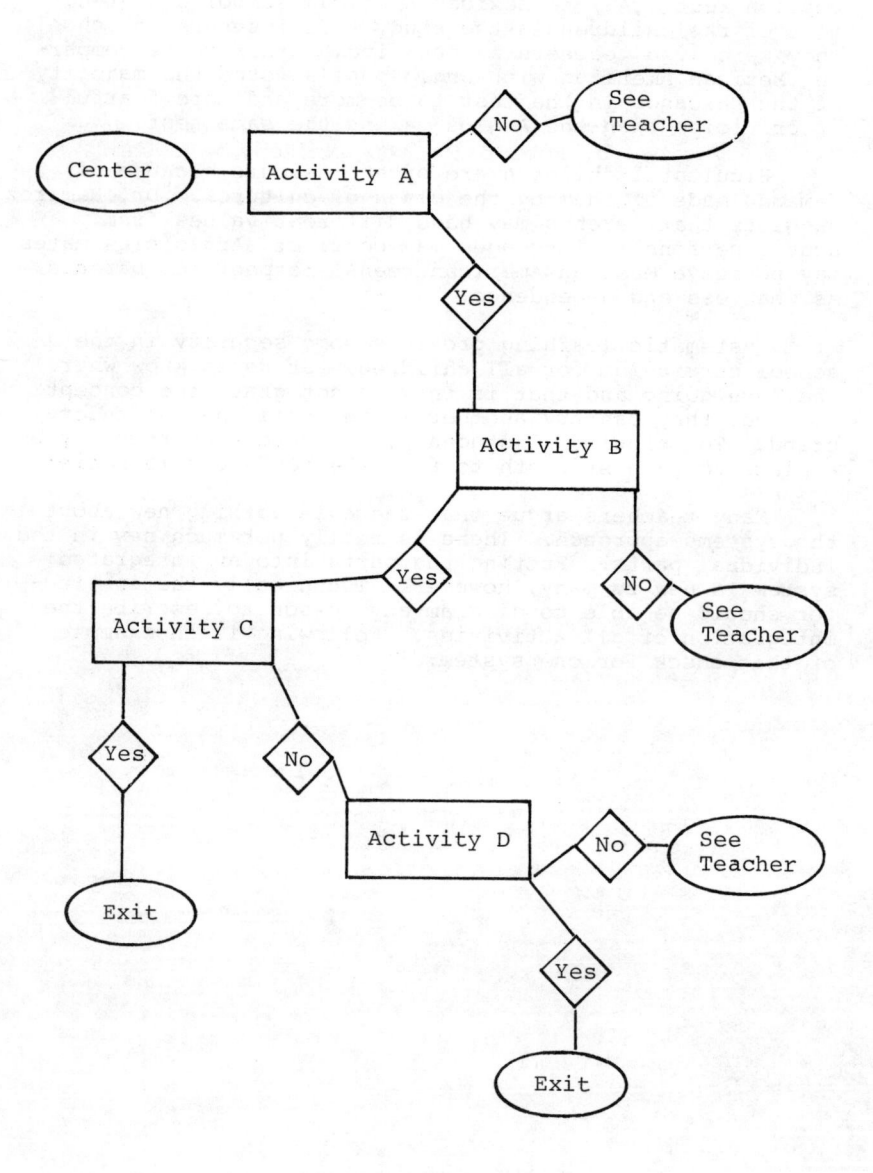

Jules Henry cites important reasons for use of systematic learning in any classroom: "Thinking would seem to involve an analytical process of some kind and also a process of synthesis. Almost none of this takes place in the elementary school."[3]

* * *

There are five general kinds of behavioral objectives described by Robert Houston and Robert Howsam:

1) the <u>cognitive</u> objective specifies intellectual and knowledge abilities students have;

2) the <u>performance</u> objective calls for behaviors the student is to perform;

3) the <u>consequence</u> or product objective states the change that will take place due to certain actions;

4) the <u>affective</u> objective specifies attitudes a student is to demonstrate;

5) the <u>expressive</u> or exploratory objective stipulates experiences the student is to undertake.[4]

* * *

After objectives are specified it is necessary to order them. This ordering, along with development of activities and assessments, becomes the module. James Cooper and Wilford Weber list seven components of most modules:

> In simple terms, an instructional module is characterized by 1) a rationale or prospectus which: a) describes the purpose and importance of the objectives of the module in empirical, theoretical, and/or practical terms: and b) places the module and the objectives of the module within the context of the total program; 2) objectives which specify the competency or competencies the student is expected to demonstrate; 3) prerequisites; that is, any competencies or experiences the student should have prior to entering into the module; 4) preassessment procedures--usually diagnostic in nature -- which provide the student with an opportunity to demonstrate mastery of the objectives and

'test out' of the module; 5) learning alternatives, which are the various instructional options available to the student and each of which is designed to contribute to his acquisition of the objectives; 6) post assessment procedures that permit the student to demonstrate achievement of the objectives; and 7) remedial procedures to be undertaken by the student who is unable to demonstrate achievement of the objectives on the post assessment.[5]

Language Learning in Content Areas

Comment

There is no definite, particular method of bilingual instruction. The major difference between a bilingual teacher and a regular elementary teacher is that the former must know language instruction methods as well as methods of content instruction.

Included in language instruction are various linguistic theories. Most of these will be described in the next chapter. Generally, though, a bilingual teacher must respect the dialect of the child and develop in step-wise lessons the languages or dialects the child is expected to speak. Those languages should be presented separately, that is, not as translations or codes of one another. A paper on the linguistic issues in bilingual education prepared by the Center for Applied Linguistics is available from CAL, 1611 N. Kent St., Arlington, Va. 22209.

Programs such as one which calls for simultaneous instruction cannot be condoned. The teachers in those programs are expected to say one phrase in English then repeat it in Spanish. It is nerve-wracking for teachers and confusing or boring to bilinguals. Monolinguals attempt to translate instead of internalizing the second language. Linguistically this method is questionable.

Every teacher is a language teacher, but in bilingual programs teachers are expected to develop the home as well as the school language.

Support

One of the main concerns in bilingual programs is that the pupils may not have time to learn everything required by the district if they learn to read in a "foreign" language.

Two separate studies indicate that bilingual program students will eventually reach and, in some cases, surpass their monolingual counterparts.

Wallace Lambert and Richard Tucker found that by the fifth grade, Anglo Canadians in French immersion bilingual classes were achieving at least as well on standardized tests in English as monolingual control groups (see p. 7).

The Edinburg, Texas, School District found that on the Texas-Mexico border the catch-up rate in reading was even faster. Children who knew no English began reading Spanish and studying English as a second language in kindergarten. By the end of the first or second grade many were reading above grade level in English.[6]

One of the most innovative studies regarding language learning in a bilingual program was made by Nelson Vieira on Portuguese bilinguals in Rhode Island. Up till that time many bilingual teachers had thought that new concepts had to be introduced in the native language. These concepts could only be expanded in the second language (SL).

Vieira writes, "We noted, however, that by their second year in the bilingual program most of the children had sufficient confidence in their SL (either English or Portuguese) to cope simultaneously with both new content and new modes of expression."[7]

The study showed that new content material introduced in the SL was transferred to and evaluated through the child's vernacular.

The Vieira study, along with more recent similar research, could be the backbone of bilingual education. The major reason is that of time. One argument against bilingual education is that there is no time to teach required content plus language development in two languages. This study shows that language development can occur along with content learning so that each concept need not be taught twice. A second reason is that language learning is often a boring process. Teachers attempt to instil new language patterns, and this results in repetition. Introducing new content is a way of stimulating children's curiosity and allowing them to learn new language patterns in a variety of ways. A third feature is that when students can see the direct application of a new skill, including language, they are more apt to see the value of that skill and enjoy it more. Fourth, linguistic principles can be applied directly to this model.

Of course, care must be taken not to expect immediate native language proficiency in the second language. Systematic presentations in simple useful structures and vocabularly with media will assure student comprehension.

Suggested Additional Readings

Baker, Eva. *Humanizing Educational Objectives*, Los Angeles: Vincent Associates, 1972. Filmstrip-tape kit.

Behavioral Objectives. Lern Associates. Slide-tape kit.

Dillman, Caroline Matheny and Harold F. Rehmlow, *Writing Instructional Objectives*. Belmont, California: Fearon, 1972.

Feure, Edgar, et al. *Learning to Be: The World of Education Today and Tomorrow*, Paris: UNESCO; London: Harrap, 1972.

Popham, James W. *Individualizing Instruction*. Los Angeles: Vincent, 1971. Filmstrip/tape kit.

Systematic Instructional Decision Making. Los Angeles: Vincent, 1967. Filmstrip tape kit.

Assessment of Competencies III

1. Design a system in which you develop one concept in both languages. Introduce the concept through activities then expand it through additional activities. Make sure each child has some activities in both languages. List the rationale, the behavioral objectives, and the methods of assessment in terms your students can understand.

2. Give at least five reasons your system will probably be more effective than a traditional lecture presentation of the same material.

Check Sheet

1. Diagram your module to check to see if it is truly a system. Your rationale must show how your module fits into the entire program where you are/might be teaching. The behavioral objectives must be written in terms that state an action that can be observed. The activities must be designed to develop the behavioral objectives you list. The assessment will be a concrete observation of the change you described in the behavioral objectives. You must provide alternate activities for students who do not attain the level of competence you determine. You must list skills a student has to have before attempting the module.

2. You must include at least 5 of the following points:

    a) Students know what is expected of them.

    b) Students have various activities in which to develop target concepts.

    c) Language is developed at the same time as content.

    d) Time is a limited factor, if one at all.

    e) Students start where they are.

    f) New material is added in a logical, progressive form.

    g) It is impossible to fail.

    h) Self-esteem is enhanced by giving the child the responsibility for learning.

    i) Learning will be assessed in changed behavior, which is observable.

    j) The module can be adapted easily to fit individual student needs.

UNIT IV

CONTENT AREAS

Upon completion of this unit you will be able to:

--List reasons for beginning language arts activities in the home dialect.
--Demonstrate knowledge of prereading skills in the child's native language.
--Describe the factors to be considered in second language instruction.
--Plan effective means of teaching concepts with consideration for the student's cultural background and language needs.
--Develop exercises or experiences that foster the child's understanding and appreciation of the unique differences in people while developing basic skills.

Language Arts

Comment

Many new reading theories are appearing because the bulk of educational concern and research deals with reading.

The bilingual teacher may also feel the push to emphasize reading. Yet in bilingual classes reading may be postponed with better results.

First of all, many immigrant or minority families have jobs that last long hours and allow little intellectual stimulation. The salaries are so low that magazines and books are a luxury in these homes. Many researchers, including S. R. Gavel,[1] have shown a high correlation between environment and reading success. A family that discusses the literature they read stimulates the young child's interest in reading. That family will also support the teacher's efforts to teach reading.

Teachers can employ the same techniques. By reading to children and discussing how they learned the material they just heard, the teacher stimulates children and introduces them to the idea that reading is a powerful tool. An aide, parent volunteer, or older student can easily assist the teacher with this task.

Second, by pleading the case of teaching two languages, the bilingual teacher can ask for more time to get reading

-39-

level up to grade level. As mentioned before (p. 33), bilingual education students may be able to attain the same grade level and even surpass monolinguals by 5th grade.

Many parents and teachers expect all students to be able to begin reading by grade 1. This is as senseless as expecting all babies to walk at nine months of age because some babies do. A test of readiness should be given to determine readiness and to prevent frustration.

Some educators concerned about language use have estimated that in the average classroom children spend about 80% of the time reading or writing and 20% of the time talking, while an average working adult reads or writes 20% of the time and talks 80% of the time.

When reading is begun, it should be in the children's home language. Not only does this strengthen their ability to learn to read at all, it also helps them speak a second language. Research seems to confirm this second factor because the child who reads is more aware of how language works.

Support

A Russian linguist has shown that teachers cannot teach concepts directly. Vygotsky claims that a teacher who tries to teach them usually accomplishes nothing but empty verbalism, a parrot-like repetition of words by the child, simulating a knowledge of the concepts by actually covering up a vacuum.[2]

* * *

Vygotsky's research is validated by Magdelen Vernon. She noted that cognitive confusion takes place when children are asked to memorize letter names and other materials that have nothing to do with the reading process. Children with reading disabilities simply have been confused. They were misled to believe that extraneous materials such as the alphabet are used in the reading task. Teachers can prevent the cognitive confusion by concentrating on the actual concepts and reasoning tasks used in reading.[3]

* * *

All research and experience indicate that a person can read, as well as speak, several languages. Nancy Modiano's research of Native Mexicans learning to read Spanish showed that the Indians who read first in their native language read better in Spanish.[4]

* * *

Reading the home dialect first leads to greater success in reading the standard language. This was shown in Sweden by Tore Osterberg in <u>Bilingualism and the First School Language: An Educational Problem Illustrated by Results from a Swedish Dialect Area.</u>[5]

Teachers of Black English speakers can cite this research when questioned about why they are teaching their children to read "bad" English.

* * *

Dr. Modiano, in a paper presented at the First Annual Conference of the Texas Association for Bilingual Education, Houston, March 23, 1973, emphasized that reading in the second language should be delayed until children have become literate in their first language. Moreover, since no language is transcribed exactly like unphonetic English--and in the United States one of the two languages will be English--difference in transcription will only serve to confuse the children, especially when they are learning to read in the Latin alphabet.

Once the teacher is certain the child will not confuse the orthography of the two languages, reading in the second language can be introduced. Dr. Modiano prefers to teach reading in the second language by having children dictate second language phrases to her. She then explains differences in orthography as problems arise. This approach lets the students discover how much they actually do know, instead of giving them complex rules they may not even need.

* * *

Robert L. Hillerich lists prereading skills that should be developed by the bilingual teacher in the child's native language.[6] These easily transfer to the second language when the child is ready to begin reading in that language, thus the child loses no time in basic skill development.

First, reading is not sounding out symbols by letter but using context for expected meaning. Children must understand their own reading as if it were read to them. This can be aided by teaching context, giving open sentences such as "When I go to the circus I see . . . ." Children can fill in the blanks with possibilities and will laugh when an incorrect word is placed in the blank. Hillerich claims that four year olds naturally become interested in context possibilities.

A second prereading skill is knowing beginning sounds. Children must learn to focus attention on one sound, they must know what "beginning" means, and they must understand same and different to be able to distinguish beginning sounds.

The third skill is knowing the written symbol for the beginning sounds practiced previously. It is more important for the prereader to know that /b/ sounds like "buh" than to know that it is called a "B." Also, if the child can associate the letter symbol with a well-known word, that sound will be more easily remembered. Hillerich has devised some flash cards for learning to read in Spanish that show the initial sound as part of a picture. The "M" is part of a mountain range, and the "F" forms part of the water and base of a fountain.

After all the prereading skills are taught, the child is shown a word while the teacher reads a sentence that ends in the word. The child combines all previous skills and "reads" the word.

* * *

Materials for reading are a problem for bilingual teachers. Those teachers should attain lists of publishers and book dealers with bilingual materials in their target language. Centers for bilingual materials have grown out of federal projects. Commercial publishers and materials resource centers are also beginning to solve the problem of the lack of reading matter. This lack hurts most programs. Native Americans have an especially difficult time, since some languages have only recently been written at all. When local dialects of international languages are considered, however, even English speakers have difficulty locating materials. Teachers of Black dialect English, for instance, find very few books available. Also, the Spanish of the Texas-Mexico border is different from those dialects of the urban areas such as Houston, New York, and Miami. Cities like Chicago, with combinations of Mexicans, Puerto Ricans, Cubans, and Latin Americans of varying generations, have problems that are most difficult unless beginning readers with similar Spanish are grouped within each class or vocabulary differences are explained prior to reading the materials.

One method of producing individualized materials for dialect speakers is the Learning Experience Activity.

e heard and practiced orally. Memory can be aided
written word association, especially for girls, who
ear to be more visually than auditorily oriented,
 written symbols in English are not regularly phonetic.
 teacher has to find the fine line between introducing
onfusing symbol and allowing memory aides.

An example of adapting methods for individual needs
 the question of pronunciation. Pronunciation is
tly a concern for older children and for adults.
ing children mimic with astonishing accuracy. This
 be a problem when the teacher's or aide's pronunci-
on retains an accent not acceptable to the dominant
ture. When students do have pronunciation diffi-
ties, the teacher should treat the sounds within the
text of the language, not as isolated phenomena, no
ter what the age. Of course, until they are 8-10
rs old, children frequently make pronunciation errors
 their native language. It would be unreasonable to
ect young children to pronounce a new language
rfectly.

Language, like content areas, must be sequenced.
ing the previous considerations, the teacher is ready
 introduce pronunciation, vocabulary, and structure
ep by step. He/she prepares lessons in which each
ncept builds on the previous one, where the introduc-
n of new items is limited and structured, where old
terial is constantly reviewed for retention, and where
e steps lead to defined outcomes for the language
arner.

Drills are often misunderstood. They are actually
petitions of phrases that build on previous knowledge,
ther transferred from the native language or learned
 the target language. This concept of drills frees
e teacher from insisting on boring, traditional drills
d provides the opportunity to create learning sessions
ich allow pupils to repeat then transform language
tterns within any context, be it games, class drills,
 peer conversations. Young children love repetitions
t need to be shown adaptions. Middle year children,
es 7-12 may be bored by repetitions and should be
ven the opportunity to practice linguistic concepts
 various forms. Exercises which include the students'
terests and personal response are more likely to
oduce second language speakers who can communicate
oficiently in the new language.

Effective communication is one of the primary goals
 all education. Finger plays, poems, skits, role
aying activities, and games can aid the children's

In LEA children draw a picture then tell the teacher, aide, or older student what is happening in the picture. The resource person writes the caption under the picture. The children practice copying the story until they are able to write it correctly. All the children take turns reading their stories within groups and then exchange papers for peer instruction in reading.

There are several ways to adapt this activity for the greatest individual benefit. For example, children who are more graphically rather than verbally oriented should be allowed to merely show their pictures until they are ready to develop their verbal potential. Another adaptation is to consider muscle coordination. Little fingers that are not able to copy the teacher's neat letters may frustrate a bright child. Plastic letters can be a solution until that child is ready to actually form the letters with a pencil.

Whatever the modification of the basic activity, the rationale for its use cannot be altered. That is, children will not be forced to read something that is outside their dialect. Children with the same language variety may be grouped together. Within their groups children then make books of the papers from the LEA, organized either by subject or child's name. These same books can then be used by other groups learning to read or speak that dialect.

The LEA method will not by itself produce successful readers unless the material is structured with scope, sequence, and objectives, just as basal readers are. The teachers guide the children by suggesting a theme, vocabulary, and/or structure to be employed.

Second Language Learning

Comment

It is often repeated that the bilingual teacher is doing the same job as any other teacher while at the same time teaching languages. The previous units have shown this to be a simplistic view. Nonetheless, it is true that bilingual teachers are expected to teach in the mother tongue and in a target or new language.

Often the target language has been called a "foreign" language. With the many native languages in this country, that term is certainly inappropriate. The most commonly used expression in bilingual programs is second language. This is also somewhat of a misnomer. In the first place it does connote secondary status, which is usually not intended by most speakers. Also the language in question may in fact be the first language learned by the student. And finally many children in bilingual programs are natively bilingual to a limited or great extent. Until the semantic issue is settled, most teachers interested in the acquisition of another language will continue to use the phrase "second language," hoping the limitations of such a term are understood.

For most bilingual teachers the target or second language is English. The unfortunate side of this is that children who know English are often left out of bilingual programs. This policy does not promote cross cultural understanding and worse, gives bilingual programs an air of compensatory education. All children should be able to reap the benefits of multicultural, bilingual education. In the ideal bilingual program all children would be completely bilingual and literate in both languages when they leave the program.

No matter what population the bilingual program serves, second language methodology is a concern. One key stage in developing methodology is studying the nature of language acquisition. In the past interference was considered a big issue in second language learning because it was believed that language skills transfer easily when both languages have similar elements. For instance, if two languages have the word order of SUBJECT, VERB, OBJECT, a student who learns the target vocabulary and structure of all three elements puts those into the correct slots and has several good sentences without ever discussing word order.

When an item does not transfer, it is said to cause interference to transfer. An English speaker attempting to learn Portuguese finds that the two English verb forms of past/nonpast do not transfer to the Romance language, which needs a separate verb form for each subject and tense. On the other hand, the English speaker will find that the characteristic "uh" sound in English will transfer to Portuguese but will cause interference with Spanish pronunciation. Recently it has been learned that most interference from native languages for non-English speakers learning English in this country occurs in pronunciation. This is compounded by the high frequency of such sounds in English as "uh," and "r".

Until recently teachers designed second language curriculum to maxamize transfer and to drill anticipated points of interference. Curriculum designers chose which points of interference to emphasize on the basis of

frequency or functional load. It was unneces[sary to]
work repeatedly on an item that would not be [used?]
because there is interference. Lately the is[sue of]
interference has been found to be of less imp[ortance]
than originally believed.

As philosophies of psychology change, at[titudes]
toward learning also change. The audiolingua[l idea of]
instilling new language habits was greatly in[fluenced by]
behavioral psychology. The resultant second [language]
methods grew out of B. F. Skinner's and his fo[llowers']
belief that language, like other cognitive pro[cesses,]
could be adapted or developed within a stimulu[s-response]
mode. Second language students were made to m[emorize]
dialogs and practice pattern drills until they [were able]
to respond automatically.

With developmental psychology and transfo[rmational]
generative linguistics came a new vision of la[nguage.]
Noam Chomsky, the leader of the transformation[al transfor-]
marions, insisted that language was a mental p[rocess and]
that, if habits grew out of the process, it wa[s due to a]
complete understanding of the functioning of t[he mind.]

The approach that grew out of the new phil[osophies of]
psychology and linguistics came to be called th[e]
cognitive method. Although some similar techni[ques are]
used and similar outcomes are desired as in the [audio-]
lingual approach, the conception of what langua[ge is]
differs. In the cognitive approach learning sh[ould be]
meaningful so that students understand what the[y are]
saying. Any visual or auditory media that have [meaning]
for the students can be employed by the teacher[including]
written words for literate pupils.

Another consideration for second language [curriculum]
development is that the methods must fit the age[s and]
interests of the students. Young children lear[n a]
language by playing than by repeating drills. S[ocial]
interaction with peers who speak the target lang[uage will]
probably develop linguistic skills much faster t[han]
lessons in the classroom. Individual children a[lso]
have varying language aptitudes and motivation f[or]
learning a second language. A child who must le[arn a]
language to survive will probably learn much fa[ster]
than a child who can see little use for the lang[uage.]
Children who are learning to read in their nativ[e]
language probably should not be allowed to see m[uch]
written second language so that they do not conf[use]
the two systems of symbols unless these sets or s[ymbols]
do not resemble each other. Older children who [rely]
on written symbols probably will need to see item[s]

-45-

communicative competence. But the most effective communication is initiated by the children themselves.

Bilingual teachers are faced with the decision as to which language varieties are to be included in the program. A large factor in the decision is that in most communities nonstandard accents in the target language are accepted or rejected more on the basis of social class than because the speaker is intelligible or not. Maurice Chevalier and Richardo Montalban receive fan mail from people intrigued by their accents while French Canadians and Mexican immigrants with similar accents are unable to find employment because they do not speak "good" English.

It will take years for bilingual education to alter the popular attitude. Bilingual teachers can, however, assure that children in a program will not suffer a similar discrimination because they speak English with a nonstandard dialect or accent. Without degrading the accent or language of the home, teachers can work toward the goal of all children speaking the prestigious dialect of the community when talking to members of the dominant culture or in formal situations, while allowing children to speak the home language with members of that same linguistic community.

Second language acquisition is most effective when other school concepts such as math and science are used as the content of the second language lesson. Often preliminary language instruction alone will be necessary to assure that children have the tools needed to be able to later grasp or reinforce the concept in the second language.

Support

Coming from the audiolingual school, Nelson Brooks, suggests the following as a guide for teaching other languages to English speakers but the same techniques can be employed in teaching English also. A language teacher should learn how to

> Introduce, sustain, and harmonize the learning of the four skills in this order: hearing, speaking, reading, and writing.
> Use--and not use--English (i.e., the native language) in the language classroom.
> Model the various types of language behavior that the student is to learn.
> Teach spoken language in dialogue form.
> Direct choral response by all or parts of the class.

Teach the use of structure through pattern practice.
Guide the student in choosing and learning vocabularly.
Get the individual student to talk.
Reward trials by the student in such a way that learning is reinforced.[8]

* * *

Some students learn better through the audiolingual pattern practice approach. Others are more successful in the cognitive style. Kenneth Chastain is one of the proponents of the cognitive approach.[9] He notes three stages through which students must pass in acquiring another language. The first stage is understanding. Students have to be aware of the meanings and relationships involved in the new material. Second is production and manipulation of structures and patterns in meaningful contexts. And third is communication, "practice in actually using previously practiced sounds, vocabulary, and structure to communicate one's thoughts to another person" (p. 411).

Each stage requires different skills and different methods. Chastain suggests that each class period be divided into three sections to accommodate for the development of those skills. The <u>preview</u> consists of explanations of the new material based on previously learned material. With more proficiency students become more able to understand these in the target language. The preview consists of about the first fourth of the language class period.

The second phase is the <u>view</u>, which comprises approximately the next half of the class. Teachers in this stage first determine if the students understood the preview. They then verify if the students can manipulate the new material. They should refrain from reexplaining the lesson and instead respond to specific questions students may have. Teachers then may require students to practice the various language skills, using the new material.

The last fourth of the class should be devoted to <u>review</u>, in which teachers relate the new materials to the students' interests. It is also the time in which students practice perfecting their new language concepts.

* * *

Wallace Lambert and G. Richard Tucker have shown that the second language can be introduced by immersing the children in that language.[10] In the St. Lambert experiment English monolingual Canadians were taught all subjects in French in kindergarten. In each of the following years language arts in English were gradually added to the curriculum. At no time did the children appear to lose any of their native language abilities when compared to English monolinguals on standardized tests. Students with the bilingual experience appeared to have gained in creativity and flexibility as well as attaining near native competence in French.

The implications of this study are great. Bilingualism can be promoted in monolinguals without loss of native language abilities.

The danger of the study is that monolinguals may use this against minority children, saying that they do not need bilingual education, that immersion in English studies should be sufficient. History has proven this answer incorrect. Teachers and administrators must bear in mind that English is the prestige language in Montreal and that the children in the six year study were from middle class homes with literate parents and English language reading material and television readily available. There were opportunities to become literate in both languages in the study, while many minority-language homes in the United States do not have middle class literate parents who encourage children to read in the native language. Television shows in languages other than English in this country usually are not as good quality, are not as frequent, and do not have the variety as shows in English.

* * *

In her textbook for teaching English as a second language to children, Louise Lancaster includes the following tips for second language teaching:

> When talking to the class, limit the English you are using to what the pupils understand rather than make excessive and possibly confusing demands on them.
> Introduce vocabulary within simple language patterns rather than as separate and isolated words.
>
> . . .
>
> Give the necessary models and guidance and correction, but do not talk too much. Your emphasis should be on the pupils doing most of the speaking.

If you isolate a sound or a word in order to correct pronunciation, always say the entire language pattern naturally and have the pupils or pupil repeat it before going on to something else.

. . .

Stay within the language limits of the lesson and the procedure without being inflexible...

In informal classroom situations, try to relate the content of a lesson to the children's natural interests in and out of school.[11]

* * *

Linguists often have stated that a teacher of a second language should employ the same principles parents use to teach babies their first language. It was only recently, however, that linguists discovered that parents do not correct the grammar of little children when they make an error. Parents only correct the content of what the child says.[12]

The implication of this discovery for teachers is that, once they know several sentence patterns, children should talk freely without teachers interrupting to interject grammatical corrections. By providing children with vocabulary within structure and with related items, by systematically presenting the structure, and by encouraging peer conversation when possible, the teacher has already minimized the student's chances for error. By listening closely to what small groups of children are attempting to communicate, the teacher can prepare more programs to correct errors through music, games, and other lessons, provided vocabulary children want to use, and guide children in what language is, communication.

Math, Science, and Health

Comment

Scientific and mathematical precepts are quite universal. There is little that is culture-bound in these disciplines.

Traditionally bilingual children have appeared better in math than in other areas. Probably they seemed better because language and culture interfere the least in mathematical equations.

Science, too often explained verbally rather than experimentally, was difficult for bilingual children because of the language problem.

Health class causes bicultural children many difficulties, for it is a cultural concern. Often health is linked with science in the school curriculum and is taught as if ideas such as the germ theory and nutrition are scientific laws. Different ethnic groups are more susceptible to specific diseases, some for known reasons, some for unknown. Some cultures attribute illness to specific organs; for example, many Hispanic people complain of liver trouble. Other cultures seem to have illusive diseases, such as the common cold of the Anglo American.

The recent battle between health food advocates and traditional nutritionists in the dominant culture exemplifies the doubts surrounding most of the health information given in grade school science or health textbooks.

Support

The most difficult part of teaching math and science in a bilingual program will probably be the limitation of the teacher's vocabulary. Most bilingual teachers have received all their education in English. Technical terms such as "cells," or "sets" are unknown to these teachers. A list of common science terminology is found in Appendix B for Spanish bilingual teachers, since Spanish is the most common language used in bilingual programs.

* * *

Dr. Atkins has received considerable criticism for his attack on traditional nutrition ideas. His major charge of interest to multicultural educators is that all of the nutrition research done in this country is sponsored by the cereal industry.[13]

Teachers should use this information only to assure themselves that they can skip the "Four Basic Food Groups" lesson and use that time for instruction of nonculturally-offensive material. Too many times the basic foods bulletin board promoters forget that beans are high in protein, that tortillas and rice contain grains, and, according to some researchers, are better foods than bread. The usual pictures of meat, fish, and loaves of white bread convince many children of other cultures that their mothers do not fix them healthy food and that, consequently, there is something wrong with their mothers, their home, and their culture.

* * *

A San Antonio physician, Dr. Ari Kiev, has investigated the role of the curandero, the healer, in that city. He has found that the curanderos are most successful in cases where Chicanos have deviated from traditional norms or have doubts about their new role in an urban, Anglo-dominated society.[14]

Teachers who dismiss the curandero's work as superstition may not only be belittling their students' culture, they may be criticizing a valuable tool for healthy integration into multicultural living.

A similar analogy can be made for other health ideas. The word "superstition" should be replaced by "beliefs" in the multicultural teacher's vocabulary. There is even a recent movement among medical researchers to return to folk medications in an attempt to cure some diseases.

Social Studies

Comment

It is in social studies that most bilingual programs dedicate much of their effort. In an attempt to build self image, the heritage of multicultural children is studied.

The danger lies in concentrating all the time on the motherland, because students rarely have much to do with that culture, because materials are often tourist-oriented and full of stereotypes, and because more can be learned about oneself and the world by comparing other peoples' values and customs with one's own.

Teachers who expect students to identify with the social studies lesson must personalize the lessons, making the target culture appear real and less exotic than it is presented in most textbooks.

Social studies can be broadened to include what the term implies, studies of societies. The idea of social studies can mean history and geography, as is usually the case, but also it can include values, dress (actual as distinguished from traditional or festive), foods, gestures, family relationships, festivals, and so on.

Interesting results often appear in classrooms with successful social studies heritage lessons. For instance, the various ethnic groups respect each other more and individual discipline problems improve as self concepts improve and as interracial dependence is demonstrated. Human beings have the same needs; the ways cultures develop means of meeting these needs makes interesting and personalized study.

Support

In his "Cross-Cultural Outline of Education", Henry criticizes the way in which most subject matter is handled. His criticism seems especially pertinent to social studies classes. "The pupil is limited in what he may learn from his teacher by the fact that the teacher often rushes through the lesson, remote from him and from the pupil either in space or time or both, and teaches subjects in which he himself is weak" (p. 284).

* * *

Carlos Cortes contrasts the traditional with the multicultural perspective in teaching social studies, particularly history.[15] Among his suggestions are the following:

1. Instead of viewing the U.S. through a political framework, it should be viewed from a geocultural perspective.

2. Instead of the traditional view of the U.S. as a collection of individuals, it should be seen as a collection of groups.

3. Instead of highlighting ethnic homogeneity, ethnic diversity should be stressed.

4. Instead of studying ethnic heroes, ethnic peoples should be exemplified.

5. Instead of considering the experience within the ethnic cultures alone, the ethnic inter-relationships with the rest of U.S. society should be studied, but without the usual view of ethnics as social problems.

Fine Arts

Comment

Art is another area where minority children traditionally have found success. Again it is a nonverbal area. Children with emotions or ideas they cannot express in "school language" often express those feelings in art class.

Music, although it is sometimes a nonverbal field, is an area with many stereotypes. Blacks are supposed to have a lot of rhythm. Hispanic children are supposed to be able to play the guitar and sing well, probably because of the flamenco guitar image of Spain, the mariachis of Mexico, and tropical groups of the Carribean.

In fact, nonverbal creative expression, which we usually label arts or crafts, and musical expression are useful tools for all teachers, and especially for teachers of children of varying backgrounds. Any concept can be reinforced through a construction, painting, or song. A teacher who plays classical or ethnic music and lets children fingerpaint, sculpt, or dance what they feel can allow expression of feelings which non-English speaking children may not be able to express verbally.

A second language is easily learned through songs. The danger lies in not preparing exercises for using the sentences learned outside of songs. For instance, children singing "Frere Jacque" will not be able to use the constructions of the song in everyday conversation without class work in which they ask classmates if they are sleeping also or without engaging in similar activities.

Support

Cri-Cri, one of Mexico's most popular singers of children's songs, has a song called the "La marcha de las letras," in which children can sing about vowels. At the same time that they are learning the names of the vowels, they have a verbal description that associates the letters with shapes they already know. Similar songs are available for children in several languages.

R. Phyllis Gelineau has listed the following ways a teacher can use music for creative expression within the basic content courses: composing words for familiar tunes, composing tunes for familiar poems, composing words and music, creating with rhythm instruments, creating with listening, and creating with body movement.[16]

The first three are easily adapted to native language arts and to second language courses through obvious techniques. Bilingual teachers may, however, also multiculturalize the other areas. For instance, rhythm instruments from various cultures may accompany poetry amd stories that deal with those cultures. The history of the instruments contributes to the students' knowledge of the history of each culture. Understanding of humanity comes through comparing instruments of several cultures to see commonalities and differences based on geography, values, and heritage.

Under the heading of "Creating with Listening," Gelineau suggests "Dramatizing listening selections heard. Painting, drawing, or using some other art medium to visually represent the music heard" (p. 307). These ideas can be integrated into the theme of a module to reinforce concepts through creative expression. They can also allow all children in the class to work on an activity together, for while the multicultural teacher should design individualized activities, the class should work as a unit on some projects in order to stimulate intergroup communication.

* * *

Contemporary popular music is one great untapped source of musical expression for classroom use. One of these musical styles that lends itself to the multicultural classroom began as a result of the minority and immigrant experiences in New York. Called "Salsa" music, it combines African, Cuban, Puerto Rican, and Spanish Harlem traditions.

The songs of "Salsa" are usually sung in Carribean dialect Spanish or Black dialect English. The music incorporates the traditions of African beat, instruments, and religious reference.[17] "Salsa" is itself a multicultural experience based on the multicultural reality of New York and other urban centers. Teachers can use it directly to teach muscle coordination, language, history, culture, musical skills, and interethnic dependence.

Integrated Teaching

Comment

The role of the bilingual teacher is to draw from knowledge of all subject matter, to make all concepts relevant in time, place, and culture to the students, and to develop the language and/or dialects the community feels are important.

The bilingual teacher, like others, needs to consider the concepts students should be able to master upon completion of the term. Just as exit requirements are important to modules, exit requirements are important to school districts, whether at the administrative, faculty, or community level. However, instead of looking at such irrelevant data as how many or which books were completed, teachers and parents must delve into the deeper issue to which concepts and skills the child should be able to employ successfully.

Educators have categorized concepts into disciplines. This practice is being challenged at all levels. Universities are successfully carrying out "interdepartmental" programs, including ethnic studies and bilingual education. Most secondary schools, however, are compartmentalized into subjects, and students rarely understand the value of the required four units of English, etc. There is some attempt to avoid the false division of disciplines in some elementary schools. The ridiculousness of the idea of subjects, especially on the primary level, is shown in the use of such terms as premath and prescience. Sample lessons for these areas often include similar concepts. For instance, the concept of same and different is included in both of these "pre" areas. "Same and different" is, however, also a "pre language arts" concept. Likewise, creativity is an important aspect of science and language arts as much as it is of music and art. The teacher who deals with concepts instead of subject matter avoids false classifications.

In bilingual programs there are two phenomena which may prevent the teacher from integrating all concepts and from using each dialect or language in its most appropriate setting. First of all, many programs are not completely bilingual. Teachers may be expected to use one subject for the minority language and to teach all other subjects in English.

The other problem is common to all teachers is that State or local education departments may require extensive records to prove that certain amounts of time were spent on each subject. The teacher must design the activities of each module to comply with the percentages of required time for each discipline. Reading math story problems, for example, can count for as much of the reading time allotment as goes into the lesson because, when a teacher uses an integrated presentation, story problems are taught for math skills, language development, reading skill, cultural content, reasoning, and so on.

These requirements are not deterents to teachers who are dedicated to providing integrated, useful, and effective means for student development. They are merely local factors to be considered in the total bilingual program, much as other community needs and requirements are considered.

Suggested Additional Readings

Baptiste, H. Prentice, Jr. ed. Multicultural Education:
A Synopsis, Houston: University of Houston Press, 1977.

Cornejo, R. J. "Reading in the Bilingual Classroom:
Methods, Approaches, Techniques & Transfer of Knowledge," Claremont Reading Conference Yearbook, XXXIX (1975), 107-12.

Goodman, K. S. The Psycholinguistic Nature of the Reading Process. Detroit: Wayne State University Press, 1968.

Johnson, Dora E. et al. eds. A Survey of Materials for the Study of the Uncommonly Taught Languages.
Arlington: Center for Applied Linguistics, 1976-77.

Kaufman, M. "Will Instruction in Reading Spanish Affect Ability in Reading English?" Journal of Reading, XI (April 1968), 521-527.

Lopez, S. H. "Children's Use of Contextual Clues in Reading Spanish." The Reading Teacher, XXX (April, 1977), 735-740.

Miller, D. D. and G. Johnson. "What We've Learned About Teaching Reading to Navajo Indians."
The Reading Teacher, 27 (March 1974), 550-554.

Olivares Arriga, María del Carmen. Enseñanza de la lectura: Procedimiento ecléctico. 3a ed. Tomo 24. Nueva Biblioteca Pedagógica. México: Eds. Oasis, 1973.

Reed, J. "Teaching Reading to Bilingual Students."
ERIC RCS Report 20 (January 1977), 346-349.

Sampson, G. P. "The Real Alternative to ESL." TESOL Quarterly, September 1977,

Segers, J. E. La enseñanza de la lectura por el método global. Buenos Aires: Kapeluz, 1958.

Smith, Frank. Understanding Reading. New York: Harcourt, Bruce & World, 1971.

Torres, Quintero, Gregorio. <u>Guía del método onomat-opéyico</u>. México: Ed. Patria, 1971.

Uribe Torres, Delores, Ana María Uribe Torres, and Ramiro Cisneros Zuckerman. <u>El método y la didáctica</u> Tomos I & II. Nueva Biblioteca Pedagógica. México: Eds. Oasis, 1970.

Assessment of Competencies IV

1. List the basic issues regarding second language or dialect instruction which concern the bilingual teacher.

2. Explain to a parent or to a student playing the role of a parent why his or her child should learn to read the language they speak at home.

3. Describe three native language activities which prepare children to read.

4. Develop the module you designed in Unit III to include activities which integrate basic skills, language arts in both language, and cultural awareness. Make sure the activities are sequenced as well as integrated.

Check Sheet

1. You should include at least five of the following ideas:

   a) Interference from the home language will probably affect the pronunciation of the new language more that it will the structure.

   b) The method depends on the psychological view of language acquisition.

   c) The age of the student determines the methods.

   d) The target language should be presented systematically.

   e) The second language is presented through the use of content area materials.

   f) The student must be allowed to talk freely in the new language.

2. Parent conferences must emphasize the positive. Many minority parents are fearful their children will not learn English. Be sure to include the research that native language arts seem to hasten second language learning. Include the idea that a child loses no time because reading skills will transfer once the child knows the second language. Reading is not sounding out words but expecting meaning; thus it should occur in the language or dialect a child knows well enough to anticipate words from the context.

3. The three major ones listed in the text were activities for teaching 1) anticipated meaning from context; 2) beginning sounds; and 3) letter sounds. There are many more prepatory activities such as training movement from right to left, teaching the concept of same and different, etc.

4. This is difficult to check on your own. Try to ascertain that the activities proceed from the known to the unknown; that the students are able to learn about their culture, preferably by comparing other cultures; that basic skills are reinforced; and that second language is taught within the concept material. Your module is in a sense the final exam and should include material you learned throughout the text.

Appendix A

BABEL TESTING AND ASSESSMENT WORKSHOP

CRITIQUE GUIDELINES

I. VOCABULARY

    a. Is the content appropriate? i.e., do the words used adequately reflect those of the age group tested? _____

    b. Degree of difficulty. Are the words used too advanced or too easy for the test level? _____

    c. Visual presentation, positioning. Are the words arranged in an easy to read fashion? _____

    d. Other _____

II. ILLUSTRATIONS

    a. Are they ambiguous? i.e., can you tell easily what each drawing is supposed to be? _____

    b. Are the pictures of good quality? i.e. appealing to children? _____

    c. Cultural implications, do they depict items naturally and easily identifiable with Chicano or Asian cultures? _____

    d. Other _____

III. DIRECTIONS

    a. Are they clear? _____

    b. Are the words used to instruct the children appropriate for their age? _____

    c. Are they very lengthy so that the point becomes unclear? _____

    d. Other _____

IV. **LAY-OUT DESIGN**

    a. Position of items - are the items placed so that they bias other items? Are they positioned sequentially or randomly?

    b. Visual effect - is the overall impact an appealing one? Are they spaced far enough apart or are the items crowded?

    c. Does one part of the test distract from another?

    d. Other?

V. **CULTURAL IMPLICATIONS**

    a. Are the items reflective of bilingual cultures?

    b. Can the illustrations and vocabulary be generalized to other cultures?

    c. Are the items "fair" to children who are bilingual/bicultural?

    d. Other

VI. **TRANSLATIONS**

    a. Are they correct?

    b. Is the vocabularly used appropriate for children?

    c. Are regional differences in language a factor?

    d. Other

VII. TIMED TESTS

    a. How significant is the
        competitive factor?   _____

    b. Is the time allowed
        appropriate for children?   _____

    c. Other?   _____

VIII. SCORING PROCEDURES

    a. Are the results meaningful?   _____

    b. Are the results clear?   _____

    c. Do the scores/results help the
        teacher to understand and help
        her students?   _____

    d. Other?   _____

IX. OTHER CONSIDERATIONS

    a. Length of test by subsection
        and total, is it fatiguing to
        children?   _____

    b. What population was the test
        normed on?   _____

    c. How large was the norming
        population?   _____

    d. Does the test appear to be
        used the way in which it was
        intended by the author?   _____

    e. Other?   _____

X. SUMMARY

    a. Does this test effectively
        evaluate the success of a
        bilingual program?   _____

b. Does the test effectively
    evaluate the potential of
    bilingual/bicultural children?

c. Does the test effectively evalu-
    ate what a child has learned in
    bilingual education classes?

d. Does the test effectively
    evaluate a bilingual child's
    I.Q.?

e. Does the test effectively
    evaluate the weaknesses of a
    bilingual program?

f. Does the test reveal to the
    teacher how she may improve
    her teaching?

g. Is taking this test of
    positive value to the child?

h. Is taking this test of negative
    value or harmful to the child.

i. Other

Appendix B

Spanish English Science Vocabulary

English	Spanish
abdomen	abdomen
absorbent	absorbente
absorption	absorción
acarus, mite	ácaro
acid	ácido
acquatic	acuático
alcholism	alcholismo
aluminum	aluminio
ameeba	amiba
amphibian	anfibio
anatomy	anatomía
anemone	anemone
anemometer	anemómetro
animal	animal
ankle	tobillo
ant	hormiga
antenna	antena
aorta	aorta
apex	ápice
appendix	apéndice
aquarium	acuario
aqueduct	acueducto
arm	brazo
aromatic	aromático
artery	arteria
articulation	articulación
asphalt	asfalto
astronomer	astrónomo
astronomy	astronomía
atmosphere	atmósfera
atom	átomo
auricle	aurícula
autumn	otoño
bacillus	baclilo
bacteria	bacteria
barometer	barómetro
beak of a bird	pico
beat	latido
begbug	chinche
beetle	escarabajo
bellowing	berrido
beverage, drink	bebidas
biennial (every 2)	bienal
bile	bilis
bird	ave

bitter	amargo
bladder	vejiga
body	cuerpo
botany	botánica
branch	rama
breast of a fowl	pechuga
brochue	bronquio
bronchitis	bronquitis
bubble	burbuja
bud	botón
bulb	bulbo
cacao	cacao
cactus	cacto
cage	jaula
calcium	calcio
calf	ternero
carbon	carbón
carnivorous (meat eating)	carnívero
cartillage	cartílago
caterpillar	oruga
cavity	caridad
cell	célula
cement	cemento
century	centuria
cerebellum (small lobe at back of brain)	cerebelo
cerebrum (main part of the brain)	cerebro
cervical	cervical
chest	pecho
cheek bone	pómulo
chew	masticar
cornea	cornea
circuit	circuito
circulation	circulación
chlorine	cloro
chlorophyll	clorofila
clavicle (collarbone)	clavícula
claws	garras
cleanliness	aseo
climbing	trepadera
clothing	vestido
clotting (coagulation)	coagulación
cluck	cloquear
coal	carbón mineral
cockroach	cucaracha
cocoon	ninfa
cold blooded	sangre fría

-69-

colon	colon
copper	cobre
coral	coral
corella (petals of a flower)	corela
cotton	algodón
crab	cangrejo
creation	creación
crustaceans	crustáceos
crystal	cristal
cultivation	cultivo
current	corriente
cyclone	ciclón
danger	peligro
deafness	sordero
degree	grado
delta	delta
dermis	dermis
desert	desierto
diameter	diámetro
diamond	diamante
diastole	diástole
digestion	digestion
dislocation	dislocacion
dissolve	disolver
domesticated	domesticado
dorsul	dorsal
drought	sequia
internal ear	oido
earthworm	lombriz
ear wax	cerumen
earthquake	terremoto
eclipse	eclipse
elbow	codo
electromagnet	electroimán
element	elemento
endecarp	endecarpe
epidermis	epidermis
epiglettis	epiglotis
equator	equador
evaporate	evaporar
expiration	espiración
external	externo
eye	ojo
eyebrow	ceja
eyelash	pestaña
eyelid	párpado
face	cara

farm	finca, granja
farmer	agricultor
femur	fémur
fertilizer	fertilizante
fingers	dedos
fibres	fibras
filter	filtro
filtration	filtración
fin	aleta
fingernail, toenail	uña
fish scales	escamas
fish	pegz
flood	inundación
fly	mosca
food	alimento
foot	pie
foot (of a hoofed animal)	pesuña
foot (of animal)	patna
flower	flor
force	fuerza
forearm	antebrazo
forehead	frente
fossil	fósil
friction	fricción
fruit	fruta, fruto
function	función
garbage	basura
garden	jardín
gastric	gástrico
germinate	germinar
gill	agalla (branquia)
gizzard	molleja
glacier	glaciar
goat	cabra
gold	oro
graft	injerto
grains	granos
granite	granito
grass, weed	hierba
gravity	gravedad
grunt	gruñido
grease	grasa
gums	encías
hail	granizo
hair	pelo
hair (on human, fruit)	vello
harvest	cosecha
head	cabeza

heart	corazón
hemp	cáñamo
hemorrhage	hemorragia
herbiverous	herbívoro
hibernate	invernar
hip	cadera
horizon	horizonte
honeycomb	panal
horn	cuerno
horse	caballo
humerus	húmero
humidity	humedad
hydrogen	hidrógeno
hydrophobia	rabia
hygiene	higiene
inanimate	inanimado
industry	industria
insect	insecto
insectiverous	insectívero
inspiration	inspiración
insulator	aislador
internal	interno
invertebrate	invertebrado
iron	hierro
joint	coyuntura
larva	larva
larynx	laringe
layer	capa
lead	plomo
leg	pierna
lever	palanca
lice	piojo
lightning	relámpago, rayo
limestone	piedra caliza
linen	lino
lip	labio
liquid	líquido
liver	hígado
livestock	ganado
locomotion	locomoción
loom	telar
lumbar	lumbar
lung	pulmón
lymph	linfa
machine	máquina
magnesium	magnesio
malaria	paludismo
mare	yegua

marsupial	marsupial
medulla	medula
meat, flesh	carne
medical	medicinal
membrane	membrana
mercury	mercurio
mesocarp	mesocarpio
metal	metal
metamorphosis	metamorfosis
metamorphic rock	roca metamórfica
microbe	microbio
microscope	microscopio
middle ear	oído medio
migrate	emigrar
mildew	moho
mineral	mineral
molar (double tooth)	muela (molar)
molecule	molécula
mosquito	zancudo
moss	musgo
mouth	boca
muscles	músculo
muscular	muscular
myopia	miopia
nape of the neck	nuca
nature	naturaleza
neck	cuello
nectar	nectar
nest	nido
neutron	neutron
nitrogen	nitrógeno
nose	nariz
nostril	fosa (nasal)
nourishment	alimentación
nucleus	nucleo
nutrition	nutrición
oil	petroleo
orange tree	naranjo
orbit	órbita
organ	órgano
organism	organismo
origin	origen
osseous, boney	oseo
outer ear	pabellón de la oreja
oviparous	ovíparo
oxygen	oxígeno
palate	paladar
pancreas	pancreas

pancreatic juice	jugo pancreático
papilla	papila
parasite	parásito
pericarium	pericardio
pericarp	pericarpio
petal	pétalo
perennial, perpetual	perenne
pentiole, leaf stalk	pecíolo
pharynx	faringe
phosphorus	fósforo
pigment	pigmento
pistil	pistilo
pituitary	pituitaria
planet	planeta
plant	planta
plasma	plasma
plastic	plástico
platelets (blood)	plaquetas
pleura	pleura
plumage	plumaje
pollen	polen
pneumonia	pulmonía
polluted	contaminado, corrompido
polyp	pólipo
pore	poro, estoma
potable	potable
powder, dust	polvo
pressure	presión
protein	proteína
proton	protón
protoplasm	protoplasma
pulley	polea
pulp	pulpa
pulse	pulso
pumice stone	piedra pomez
pupil of the eye	pupila
purify	purificar
pylerus	pilero
radiation	radiación
radicle, rootlet	radícula
rainbow	arco iris
red cells	glóbulos rojos
reproduction	reproducción
reptile	reptil
respiration, breathing	respiración
retina	retina
rib	costilla
ringworm (of the scalp)	tiña

rocket	cohete
rodent	roedor
root	raiz
rotula	rótula
rough	ásoera
ruminant (cud chewing)	rumiante
sacrum	sacro
salamander	salamandra
salt	sal
sand	arena
saliva	saliva
salivary glands	glándulas salivares
sap	savia
satellite	satélite
savage	salvaje
science	ciencias
screw	tornillo
seaweed	alga marina
sebaccous gland	glándulas sebaceosas
seed	semilla
segment	segmento
seismograph	sismógrafo
sensation	sensación
sensory	sensor
sense	sentido
sepal	sépalo
septum (of the nose)	tabique
sewage	aguas de albañal
shell	cáscara
shoulder	hombro
shrub	arbusto
sight, vision	visión, vista
silk	seda
silicon	silicio
sisal, hemp	sisal
skin	piel
skin, leather	cuero
skeleton	esqueleto
skull	casco
smell (sense of)	olfato
smoke	humo
snail, cochlea (of the ear)	caracol
snout	hocico
sodium	sodio
sowing seeding	siembra
solar	solar
solid	solido
sound	sonido

sound wave	onda sonora
species	especie
spider	araña
spine	columna
star fish	estrella del mar
stem	tallo
sterilize	esterilizar
sternum	esternón
stimulating	estimulantes
sting	aguijón
stolon	estolón
stomach	estómago
stone	piedra
storm	tempestad
subterranean	subterraneo
sulphur	azufre
sweat	sudar
sweat, perspiration	sudor
sweat glands	glándulas suderíferas
sweet	dulce
system	sistema, aparato
systole	sistole
tail	rabo
taste	sabor, gusto
tear	lágrima
temperature	temperatura
tendon	tendón
terrestrial	terrestre
textile	textil
thermometer	termómetro
thorax	tórax
thorn	espina
thunder	trueno
tobacco	tabaco
topsoil	suelo
tornado	tornado
tree	árbol
tree nursery	almácigo
tricuspid	tricuspido
trunk	tronco
tuberolo	tubérculo
tuberculosis	tuberculosis
universe	universo
vaccine	vacuna
valve	válvula
vapor	vapor
vegetable	hortaliza
vein	vena
ventriole	ventrículo

vertebra	vértebra
vertebrate	vertebrado
vestibule of the ear	vestíbulo
vibrate	vibrar
virus	virus
vitamin	vitamina
viviparous	vivíparo
volcano	volcán
warm	gusano
wasp	avispa
wasp's nest	avispero
weaving	tejido
white cells	glóbulos blancos
whooping cough	tos ferina
winch, lathe	torno
wind	viento
wing	ala
winter	invierno
wool	lana
wrist	muñeca
xiphoio (lower breast bone)	xifoides
zoology	zoología

REFERENCES

Introduction

1. Patricia Baca de McNicholas, "A Comparison of the Perceptions Toward Bilingual Education by Parents, Administrators, and Teachers in Two Urban Settings" (Unpublished diss., University of Houston, 1977).

Unit I

1. Rpt. in Theodore Andersson and Mildred Boyer, Bilingual Schooling in the United States, II (Austin: Southwest Educational Development Laboratory, 1970), p. 8.

2. Joshua Fishman, "Bilingual Education in Socio-Linguistic Perspective" (1970), ERIC document ED 040404. See also Wallace Lambert, "A Social Psychology of Bilingualism," Journal of Social Issues, XXII, 2 (1967), 91-110.

3. William F. Mackey, "A Typology of Bilingual Education," in Joshua Fishmen, ed., Advances in the Sociology of Language, Vol. II (The Hague: Mouton, 1972) pp. 413-432.

4. Texas Education Agency. "Statewide Design for Bilingual Education," Pamphlet from the Office of International and Bilingual Education.

5. National Education Association, "The Invisible Minority," in John H. Burma, ed., Mexican Americans in the United States: A Reader (Cambridge: Schenkman, 1970), p. 5.

6. Robert Rosenthal and Leonore F. Jacobson, "Teacher Expectations for the Disadvantaged," Scientific American, CCX VIII, 4 (April, 1968), 6.

7. Clark S. Knowlton, "Bilingualism: A Problem or an Asset?" Memeo, n.d., pp. 2, 5.

8. Chester C. Christian, Jr., "The Acculturation of The Bilingual Child," Modern Language Journal, XLIX (Mar. 1965), 164.

9. Miles V. Zintz, Education Across Cultures (Dubuque: Kendall/Hunt, 1963), pp. 135-136.

10. A. Bruce Gaarder, "Linkages Between Foreign Language Teaching and Bilingual Education," in J. E. Alatis and Kristie Twaddell, eds., English as a Second Language in Bilingual Education (Washington: TESOL, 1976), pp. 199-203.

11. Wallace E. Lambert and G. Richard Tucker, "The Benefits of Bilingualism," Psychology Today, Sept. 1973, 89.

12. Wilder Penfield, "The Uncommitted Cortex," Atlantic Monthly, 214 (July, 1964), 77.

Unit II

1. William Madsen, Mexican Americans of South Texas (New York: Holt, Rinehart, and Winston, 1964).

2. Celia Stopnicka Heller, Mexican-American Youth: Forgotten Youth at the Crossroads (New York: Random House, 1968).

3. Herminio C. Rios, "Preface," Voices: Readings from "El Grito," ed. Octavio I. Romano- V. (Berkeley: Quinto Sol, 1971), pp. 6-7.

4. Octavio I. Romano- V., "The Anthropology and Sociology of the Mexican-Americans: The Distortion of Mexican-American History," Voices, pp. 35-36.

5. Oscar Lewis, Five Families: Mexican Case Studies in the Culture of Poverty (New York: Basic Books, 1959).

6. David Lopez-Lee, "On Categorizaitons: Know Your Jaundiced Eye," The Journal of Comparative Cultures, 1, 2, 114.

7. Women on Words and Images, "Some Criteria for Evaluating Materials," in Emma Willard Task Force on Education, Sexism in Education, 3rd ed. (Minneapolis: The Task Force, 1972), p. 26.

8. Maria Swanson, paper presented at the Texas Foreign Language Association, Beaumont, October, 1972.

9. Wallace Lambert, "A Social Psychology of Bilingualism," Journal of Social Issues, XXII, 2 (1967), 93-98.

10. Gussie A. Trahan, "The Relationship of Dogmatism in Preservice and Inservice Teachers to their Willingness to Describe Afro and Mexican American Women When Given Limited Data" (unpublished diss., University of Houston, 1976).

11. Bay Area Bilingual Education League, Bilingual Testing and Assessment (Berkeley: BABEL, 1972).

12. Pauline S. Sears and David H. Feldman, "Teacher Interactions with Boys and with Girls," in Judith Stacey et al., eds., And Jill Came Tumbling After: Sexism in American Education (New York: Dell, 1974), p. 153.

13. Carol Tittle, "The Use and Abuse of Vocational Tests," in Stacey, et al., p. 241.

14. Manuel Ramirez, "Evaluation and Assessment: The Assault on the Chicano's Wounded Knee," paper presented at the First Annual Multilingual Multicultural Conference, San Diego, April, 1973.

15. Reported in Miles Zintz, p. 254.

Unit III

1. Benjamin S. Bloom, J. Thomas Hastings and George F. Madaus, Handbook of Formative and Summative Evaluation of Student Learning (New York: McGraw-Hill, 1971).

2. Manuel Ramirez, "The Schools and Alienation of the Mexican-American Student," in Ernest M. Bernal, Jr., ed. The San Antonio Conference on Bilingual-Bicultural Education--Where Do We Go From Here? (San Antonio: Bureau of Educational Development, U.S. Office of Education and St. Mary's University, March 28-29, 1969), pp. 49-57.

3. Jules Henry, "A Cross-Cultural Outline of Education," Current Anthropology, 1, 274.

4. Robert Houston and Robert Howsam, "Change and Challenge," in Competency Based Teacher Education: Progress, Problems, and Prospects, eds. Robert Houston and Robert Howsam (Palo Alto: Science Research Assoc., 1972) pp. 1-16. Rpt. in Wilford A. Wever et al., eds., A Guide to Competency Based Teacher Education (Westfield, Texas: Competency Based Instructional Systems, 1973), issue 21 (n.p.).

5. James Cooper and Wilford Weber, "A Competency-Based Systems Approach to Education," in James M. Cooper et al., eds., Competency Based Teacher Education: A Systems Approach to Program Design (Berkeley: McCutchan Pub., 1973), pp. 7-18. Rpt. in Weber, et al, Issue 24.

6. "Teaching Reading to Spanish Speakers," film produced by Educational Resource Center, Region I, Edinburg, Texas, 1974.

7. Nelson Vieira, "The Bilingual Classroom: A Clinic for Foreign Language Teaching," Hispania, LIV, 4 (Dec., 1971), 905.

Unit IV

1. S. R. Gavel, "June Reading Achievement of First-grade Children," Journal of Education, Boston U., 140 (1958), 37-43.

2. Lev. S. Vygotsky, Thought and Language (Cambridge: MIT Press, 1962).

3. Magdelen Vernon, Backwardness in Reading (London: Cambridge U. Press, 1957).

4. Nancy Modiano, "A Comparative Study to Two Approaches to the Teaching of Reading in the National Language" (diss., New York University School of Education, 1966).

5. Tore Osterberg, Bilingualism and the First School Language: An Educational Problem Illustrated by Results from a Swedish Dialect Area (Umea, Sweden: Vasterbottens Tryckeri AB., 1961).

6. Robert L. Hillerich, "Beginning Reading for Spanish Speaking Children," Timely Topics, VII, 2 (Jan.-Feb., 1974).

7. Noam Chomsky, "Review of Verbal Behavior by B. F. Skinner," Language, 35, 26-58.

8. Nelson Brooks, Language and Language Learning: Theory and Practice (New York: Harcourt, Brace & World, 1960), p. 139.

9. Kenneth Chastain, Developing Second Language Skills: Theory to Practice, 2nd ed. (Chicago: Rand McNally, 1976).

10. Wallace Lambert and G. Richard Tucker, <u>Bilingual Education of Children: The St. Lambert Experiment</u> (Rowley, Mass.: Newbury House, 1972).

11. Louise Lancaster, <u>Teacher's Guide to "Introducing English"</u> (Boston: Houghton Mifflin, 1970), xi-xii.

12. G. Richard Tucker, "Myths and Realities of Bilingual Education: Observations from the Montreal Experience." Paper presented at the Fourth Annual International Bilingual/Bicultural Education Conference, Chicago, May 23, 1975.

13. Robert C. Atkins, <u>Dr. Atkins Diet Revolution</u> (New York: Bantam, 1977).

14. Ari Kiev, Curanderismo: <u>Mexican-American Folk Psychiatry</u> (New York: Free Press, 1972).

15. Carlos Cortes, "New Concepts for Teaching the Multicultural Experience," in <u>Multicultural Education: Theory, Issues and Application</u>, ed. by H. Prentice Baptiste, Jr., Carlos Cortes and Judith Walker (in press).

16. Phyllis Gelineau, <u>Experiences in Music</u> (New York: McGraw-Hill, 1970).

17. Robert Farris Thompson, "Neuva York's Salsa Music," <u>Saturday Review</u>, June 28, 1975, pp. 33-35.

Bibliography

Anderson, Theodorr & Mildred Boyer. Bilingual Schooling in the United States, II Austin: Southwest Educational Development Laboratory, 1970.

Atkins, Robert C. Dr. Atkin's Diet Revolution, New York: Bantam, 1977.

Baca de McNicholas, Patricia. "A Comparison of the Perceptions toward Bilingual Education by Parents, Administrators, & Teachers in Two Urban Settings." Unpublished dissertation, University of Houston, 1977.

Baker, Eva. Humanizing Educational Objectives. Los Angeles: Vincent Associates, 1972.

Baptiste, H. Prentice, Jr., ed. Multicultural Education: A Synopsis. Houston: University of Houston Press, 1977.

Bay Area Bilingual Education League. Bilingual Testing and Assessment. Berkeley: BABEL, 1972.

Bloom, Benjamin S., Thomas Hastings, and George F. Madaus. Handbook of Formative and Summative Evaluation of Student Learning New York: McGraw-Hill Book Company, 1971.

Brooks, Nelson. Language and Language Learning: Theory and Practice. New York: Harcourt, Brace & World, 1960.

Burma, John H., ed. Mexican-Americans in the United States: A Reader. Cambridge, Mass.: Schenkman Publishers, 1970.

Cabrera, Y. Arturo. Emerging Faces: The Mexican-Americans. Dubuque: Brown, 1971.

Carlson, Ruth Kearney. Emerging Humanity: Multi-Ethnic Literature for Children and Adolescents. Dubuque: Brown, 1972.

Carter, Thomas P. Mexican Americans in School: A History of Educational Neglect. New York: College Entrance Examination Board, 1970.

Chastain, Kenneth. *Developing Second Language Skills: Theory to Practice*, 2nd ed. Chicago: Rand McNally, 1976.

Chomsky, Noam. "Review of *Verbal Behavior* by B. F. Skinner," *Language*, 35, 26-58.

Christian, Chester C. Jr., "The Acculturation of the Bilingual Child," *Modern Language Journal*, XLIX (March, 1965) pp. 160-165.

Christian, Jane and Chester C. Christian, Jr. "Spanish Language and Culture in the Southwest." In Joshua A. Fishman, et al. *Language Loyalty in the United States: The Maintenance and Perpetuation of Non-English Mother Tongues by American Ethnic and Religious Groups*. The Hague: Mouton, 1966.

Cooper, James & Wilford Weber. "A Competency-Based Systems Approach to Education." In James M. Cooper et al., eds., *Competency Based Teacher Education: A Systems Approach to Program Design*, Berkeley: McCutchan Publishing, 1973, pp. 7-18. Rpt. in Wilford Weber, et al. *A Guide to Competency Based Teacher Education*. Westfield, Texas: Competency Based Instructional Systems, 1973, Issue 24.

Cornejo, R. J. "Reading in the Bilingual Classroom: Methods, Approaches, Techniques and Transfer of Knowledge." *Claremont Reading Conference Yearbook*, XXXIX (1975), 107-112.

Cortes, Carlos. "New Concepts for Teaching the Multicultural Experience." In H. Prentice Baptiste, Jr., Carlos Cortes, & Judith Walker, eds., *Multicultural Education: Theory, Issues and Application* (in press).

Dillman, Caroline Matheny & Harold Rehmlow. *Writing Instructional Objectives*. Belmont, California: Fearon, 1972.

Emma Willard Task Force on Education, *Sexism in Education*. 3rd ed. Minneapolis: The Task Force, 1972.

Fishman, Joshua, "Bilingual Education in Socio-Linguistic Perspective", ERIC document ED 040404, (1970).

Feure, Edgar, et al. *Learning to Be: The World of Education Today and Tomorrow*. Paris: UNESCO; London: Harrap, 1972.

Forbes, Jack D., ed. "Education, the Continuing Struggle." Chapter V in *Aztecas del Norte: The Chicanos of Aztlan*. Greenwich, Conn.: Fawcett, 1973.

Gaarder, A. Bruce. "Linkages Between Foreign Language Technology & Bilingual Education" in L. E. Alatis & K. Twadell ets., *English as a 2nd Language in Bilingual Education* (D.C.: TESOL, 1976), pp. 199-203.

--. Teaching the Bilingual Child." *Modern Language Journal*, XLIX (March 1965), 165-175.

Gavel, S. R. "June Reading Achievement of First-grade Children." *Journal of Education*, Boston, U., 140 (1958), 37-43.

Gelineau, R. Phyllis. *Experiences in Music*. New York: McGraw-Hill, 1970.

Goodman, K. S. *The Psycholinguistic Nature of the Reading Process*. Detroit: Wayne State University Press, 1968.

Heller, Celia Stopnicka. *Mexican-American Youth: Forgotten Youth at the Crossroads*. New York: Random House, 1968.

Henry, Jules. "A Cross-Cultural Outline of Education." *Current Anthropology*. 1, 274-83.

Hillerich, Robert. "Beginning Reading for Spanish-Speaking Children," *Timely Topics*, VII, 2 (January-February, 1974).

Houston, Robert & Robert Howsam, "Change and Challenge." In *Competency Based Teacher Education: Progress, Problems, and Prospects*. Ed. Robert Houston and Robert Howsam. Palo Alto: Science Research Assoc., 1972. pp. 1-16. Rpt. in Wilford A Wever et al., eds., *A Guide to Competency Based Teacher Education*. Westfield, Texas: Competency Based Instructional Systems, 1973. Issue 21 (n.p.).

Jacobson, Leonore F. & Robert Rosenthal, "Teacher Expectations for the Disadvantaged." *Scientific American*, CCXVIII, 4 (April, 1968), pp. 19-23.

Johnson, Dora E. et al., eds. *A Survey of Materials for the Study of the Uncommonly Taught Languages*. Arlington: Center for Applied Linguistics, 1976-77.

Juhl, Joya, Paul C. and Juan Rosales. <u>Some Thoughts,
Some Activities: Sensitivity Experiences for the
Teacher of Mexican American Children in the Ele-
mentary School.</u>

Kaufman, M. "Will Instruction in Reading Spanish
Affect Ability in Reading English?" <u>Journal of
Reading</u>, IX (April 1968), 521-527.

Kiev, Ari. Curanderismo: <u>Mexican-American Folk
Psychiatry</u>. New York: Free Press, 1972.

Knowlton, Clark S., "Bilingualism: A Problem or an
Asset?" Mimeographed. n.d.

Lambert, Wallace. "A Social Psychology of Bilingualism."
<u>Journal of Social Issues,</u> IIII, 2 (1967), 91-110.
pp. 89-94.

-- <u>Bilingual Education of children. The St. Lambert
Experiment.</u>
Rowley, Mass.: Newbury House, 1972.

Lancaster, Louise. <u>Introducing English</u>. Teacher's
Guide. Boston: Houghton Mifflin, 1970.

Lewis, Oscar. "Five Families: Mexican Case Studies in
<u>The Culture of Poverty</u>. New York: Basic Books, 1959.

Lopez, S. H. "Childresn's Use of Contextual Clues in
Reading Spanish." <u>The Reading Teacher</u>, XXX (April
1977), 735-740.

Lopez-Lee, David. "On Categorizations: Know your
Jaundiced Eye." <u>The Journal of Comparative Cultures</u>,
1, 2, 113-121.

Mackey, William F. "A Typology of Bilingual Education."
In Joshua Fishman, ed. <u>Advances in the Sociology of
Language</u>. Vol. II The Hague: Mouton, 1972. pp.
413-32.

Madsen, William. <u>Mexican Americans of South Texas</u>.
New York: Holt, Rinehart, and Winston, 1964.

Mercer, Jane. "Multicultural Assessment Procedures for Chicanos in Public School." Paper presented at the First Annual International Multilingual Multicultural Conference, San Diego, April 1972.

Miller, D. D. and G. Johnson. "What We've Learned About Teaching Reading to Navajo Indians." The Reading Teacher, 27 (March 1974), 550-554.

Modiano, Nancy. "A Comparative Study to Two Approaches to the Teaching of Reading in the National Language." Unpublished diss. New York University School of Education, 1966.

Montiel, Miquel. "The Social Science Myth of the Mexican American Family." In Octavio I. Romano-V., ed. Voices: Readings from "El Grito". Berkeley: Quinto Sol, 1971, pp. 40-47.

Moreno, Steve. "Problems Related to Present Testing Instruments," in Voices: Readings from "El Grito". Ed. Octavio I. Romano-V. Berkeley: Quinto Sol, 1971, pp. 135-39

National Education Association. "The Invisible Minority." In John H. Burma, ed., Mexican Americans in the United States: A Reader. Cambridge: Schenkman, 1970.

Olivares Arriga, María del Carmen. Enseñanza de la lectura: Procedimiento ecléctico. 3a ed. Tomo 24. Nueva Biblioteca Pedagógica. México: Eds. Oasis, 1973.

Osterberg, Tore. Bilingualism and the First School Language: An Educational Problem Illustrated by Results from a Swedish Dialect Area. Umea, Sweden: Vasterbottens Tryckeri AB., 1961.

Palomares, Uvaldo and Miquel P. Trujillo. "Examination of Assessment Practices and Goals and the Development of a Pilot Intelligence Test for Chicano Children." First Quarterly Project Report, Office of Economic Opportunity Grant. Washington: OEO, October, 1971.

Penfield, Wilder, "The Uncommitted Cortex," Atlantic Monthly, 214 (July, 1964), pp. 77081.

Popham, James W. *Individualizing Instruction*. Los Angeles: Vincent, 1971.

Ramirez, Manuel. "Evaluation and Assessment: The Assault on the Chicano's Wounded Knee, "Paper presented at the First Annual Multilingual Multicultural Conference, San Diego, April, 1973.

- - "The Schools and Alienation of the Mexican-American Students." *The San Antonio Conference on Bilingual-Bicultural Education--Where Do We Go From Here?* San Antonio: Bureau of Educational Development, U. S. Office of Education and St. Mary's University, March. 28-29, 1969, pp. 49-57.

Reed, J. "Teaching Reading to Bilingual Students." ERIC/RCS Report 20 (January 1977), 346-349.

Rios, Herminio C., "Preface,: *Voices: Readings from "El Grito."* Ed. Octavio I. Romano-V. Berkely: Quinto Sol, 1971, pp. 6-7

Romano-V., Octavio I. "The Anthropology and Sociology of the Mexican-Americans: The Distortion of Mexican-American History." In *Voices: Readings F "El Grito."* Ed. Octavio I. Romano-V. Berkeley: Quinto Sol, 1971, pp. 35-36.

Sampson, G. P. "The Real Alternative to ESL." *TESOL Quarterly*. September 1977. 241-55.

Saville, Muriel R. and Rudolph C. Troike, *A Handbook of Bilingual Education*. ERIC document ED 035 877.

Sears, Pauline S. and David H. Feldman "Teacher Interactions with Boys and with Girls" in Judith Stacey et al., eds. *And Jill Came Tumbling After: Sexism in American Education* New York: Dell, 1974, p. 153.

Segers, J. E. *La enseñanza de la lectura por el método global*. Buenos Aires: Kapeluz, 1958.

Smith, Frank, *Understanding Reading*. New York: Harcourt, Brace and World, 1971.

Systematic Instructional Decision Making. Los Angeles: Vincent, 1967.

"Teaching Reading to Spanish Speakers," film produced by Educational Resource Center, Region I, Edingburg, Texas, 1974.

Texas Education Agency. "Statewide Design for Bilingual Education," Pamphlet from Office of International & Bilingual Education. Austin: State of Texas, n.d.

Thompson, Robert Farris. "Nueva York's Salsa Music." Saturday Review, June 28, 1975.

Tittle, Carol. "The Use and Abuse of Vocational Tests," in Judith Stacey et al., eds., And Jill Came Tumbling After: Sexism in American Education. New York: Dell, 1974, p. 241.

Torres Quintero, Gregorio. Guía del método onomatopéyico. Mexico: Ed. Patria, 1971.

Trahan, Gussie A. "The Relationship of Dogmatism in Preservice and Inservice Teachers to their Willingness to Describe Afro & Mexican American Wormen When Given Limited Data." Unpublished dissertation. University of Houston, 1976.

Tucker, Richard G. "Myths and Realitites of Bilingual Eudcation: Observations from the Montreal Experience." Paper presented at the Fourth Annual International Bilingual/Bicultural Education Conference, Chicago, May 1975.

Uribe Torres, Delores, Ana María Uribe Torres and Ramiro Cisneros Zuckerman. El método y la didáctica. Tomos I & II. Nueva Biblioteca Pedagógica. México: Eds. Oasis, 1970.

The U. S. Commission on Civil Rights on Mexican American Education. The Unfinished Education. Washington, D. C.: U. S. Printing Office, 1971.

--. Teachers and Students: Differences in Interaction Between Teachers with Mexican American Students and North American or Anglo Students. Washington, D. C.: U. S. Printing Office, 1973.

--. A Better Chance to Learn: Bilingual Bicultural Education. Washington, D. C., 1974.

Vernon, Magdelen. *Backwardness in Reading*. London: Cambridge University Press, 1957.

Vieira, Nelson. "The Bilingual Classroom: A Clinic for Foreign Language Teaching," *Hispania*, LIV, 4 (December, 1971), P. 905.

Vygotsky, Lev S. *Thought and Language*. Cambridge: MIT Press, 1962.

Wofram, Walt and Ralph W. Fasold. *The Study of Social Dialects in American English*. Englewood Cliffs, N. J.: Prentice Hall, 1974.

Zintz, Miles V. *Education Across Cultures*. Dubuque: Kendall/Hunt, 1963.

ABOUT THE AUTHOR

Judith Walker was born in 1943 in Kansas. She studied Spanish education at the University of Kansas 1961-64.

In 1965 she attended an NDEA Institute in foreign language education at Rice University in Houston. That school year she participated in Houston's FLES program teaching Spanish to third through sixth grades. She attended another NDEA Institute in Spain. After teaching Spanish in two Houston high schools, she was awarded an NDEA fellowship to pursue doctoral studies at the University of Florida. Her work there consisted of studying Spanish and Portuguese languages and literature, and she carried out a sociological study in Buenos Aires. Her dissertation was "The Influence of Gonzalez Prada on Modern Peruvian Essayists."

Dr. Walker returned to Houston to teach at Dominican College in 1972. There she developed the first competency-based bilingual teacher education program in Texas. She began to investigate aspects of Mexican American culture and its influence on bilingual education. She also volunteered as an English-as-a-Second Language teacher.

In 1975 she started teaching at the University of Houston, where she developed the Masters-level bilingual program. She is currently teaching bilingual education and investigating ESL for Venezuelan children and some neurological aspects of bilingualism.

DATE DUE

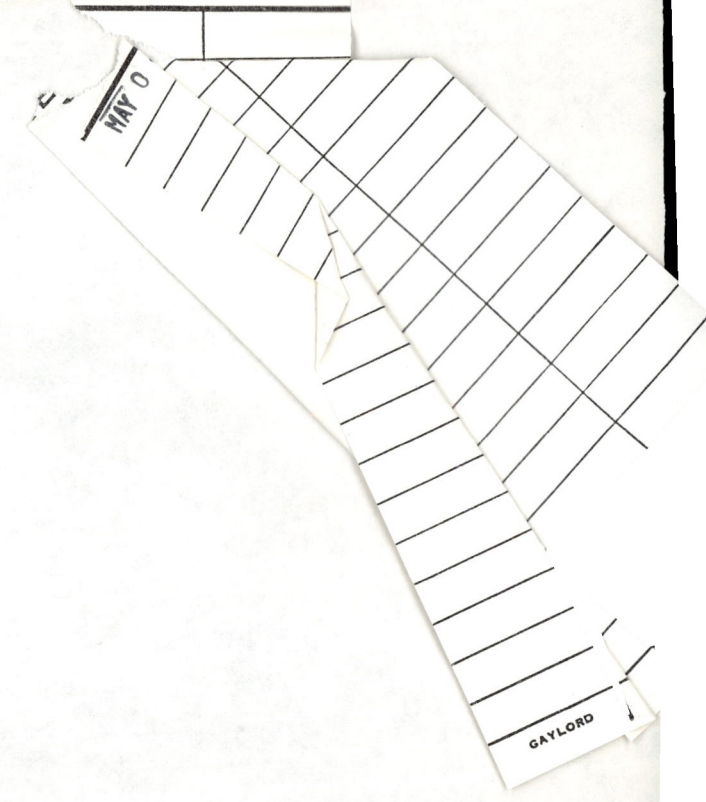

MAY 0

GAYLORD